CONCERNING SUBUD

Concerning Subud
Second edition, revised by the author

J.G. Bennett

Published by The J.G. Bennett Foundation

Series Editor: Ben Bennett

CONCERNING SUBUD

J.G. BENNETT

REVISED EDITION

WITH ADDITIONAL MATERIAL

Publisher's note:

Although *Concerning Subud* was J.G. Bennett's best-selling book, he refused after the second edition was sold out, to allow his publisher to make any further impressions. The reasons for his decision are not known. Bennett left the Subud Brotherhood in 1960 although he continued until the end of his life to receive letters from readers of this book. Originally, the members of his Estate opted to respect his wishes with regard to publication, but after the passage of more than 40 years, it is felt that the text will be of interest to researchers. The second edition contained some modifications from the first, and it is this edition which is published herewith. The format and content of the original text have been preserved from the published text as far as possible. It seems unlikely that present-day practitioners of Subud will recognise some of the descriptions as credible or valid, nor credit some of the assertions made in this book. Many may find the connection to Gurdjieff asserted by the author, to be irrelevant and even distasteful. However others will find this history to be of interest and it is for those readers that this book is intended.

Contents

PREFACE TO THE
SECOND EDITION

Little more than a hundred days have passed since this
book was first published, and during that time much has
happened. Subud has completed its first circuit of the earth,
and I have been able to witness its progress in the United
States, Australia, Indonesia, Singapore and Ceylon. There are
now active Subud centres, branches and individual members
in more than half the countries of the world. In London alone,
letters are being received at the rate of more than two hundred
a week and nearly all of them express the sense of need and
urgency with which the prospect of a positive spiritual action
is welcomed by people of all races and religions. An account
of my own observations has been added to Chapter 3, and I
have also made a few corrections of fact in the light of fuller
information about the origins of Subud.

I have removed several paragraphs from the Foreword. As
often happens, in trying to avoid offence I have tended to create
confusion. There is no need to look for a causal or historical link
between Subud and Gurdjieff's System, the Tibetan Teachings,
or any other of the movements that have prepared the coming
of the new epoch. Whether or not the coming of Subud was
foreseen and predicted by Gurdjieff is irrelevant to the fact
that the psychological contents and methods of his system and
Subud are mutually complementary. The two fit like the two
halves of an apple. This can easily be verified by anyone who
will take the trouble to study Pak Subuh's own book Susila
Budhi Dharma and the substance of explanatory talks he has
given in several countries in parallel with Gurdjieff's own
writings and lectures. Students of the latter have for the most
part failed to remark that - unlike his commentators - he avoids
explicit reference to the potentialities for human experience
and development beyond the level of the normal balanced man.

Similarly, Pak Subuh, writing of the forces that act in man's life, cuts short his exposition at the human forces, designating the three superhuman levels, but declining to enlarge upon their nature. The possibility for man to evolve beyond the level of normal humanity is not denied, but there is no profit in attempting to describe in language forms of experience and modes of action that are beyond the reach of the mind. The evidence that such experience and such action are real and do occur here and now on the earth is to be found in the results.

Innumerable events connected with Subud have occurred that only can be accounted for either by stretching the arm of coincidence to circle the world or by admitting the action of a Directive Consciousness far beyond the mind of man. I hope that it may be possible to collect and record these events in a later book. Hundreds of men and women who have come to Subud are aware of a directive, dynamic pattern that is shaping their lives and have no doubt that this action is a direct consequence of their association with Subud. It is impossible to convey to others a private conviction that has grown out of the knowledge that a man has of his own life. He can see for himself that something new has happened to him, not only in his inner state but also in his outward circumstances, and he can be sure that this could not have happened fortuitously or as a result of his own sagacity. He can see a change of 'shape' and very often others who know him well can see this change also; but neither he nor they could convey this in a few sentences. Autobiographies are needed and not everyone is competent to write one; but I know that several people have undertaken the task and if, as I hope, some of these are published, they will be more convincing than anything that I can convey at second hand.

The general conclusion to which I have come is that there is a Conscious Power now working in the world, and that Subud is a means whereby individuals and communities can come into contact with that Power, to be helped by it and eventually to serve it. The action of the Power is observable in

2

many forms and each one of us is naturally inclined to regard the manifestation to which we are nearest as the principal and, sometimes, even the only true one.

This raises the question of the connection between Subud and organized religion. We are not yet wholly free from the old intolerance which regarded all faiths but our own as heresy or worse. It is still, for many of us, hard to admit the possibility that spiritual gifts may come to us from outside our own communion. Yet times have greatly changed and there are millions throughout the world ready to accept that faith in God and love towards man are the essentials of religion and that men should be free to choose the form of their worship. We can accept without reservation Pak Subuh's assurance that Subud is not a new religion and that it does not take the place of the faith we have each received from our parents or the society to which we belong. Subud is a means whereby faith can be renewed and I have seen ample proof that as a means it is effectual. Many Christians who had ceased from religious observance have, through Subud, been brought back to their Church and especially to the Sacraments. Not only this: priests of more than one denomination have sought and found in Subud a renewal of strength. Others have written approvingly of Subud and of their hope that it will be taken seriously by the Churches as an ally in the struggle with the material forces that threaten mankind.

We are still at the beginning and must be prepared to regard Subud as an experiment with great potentialities and as such be ready to wait patiently for further evidence. Pak Subuh himself has said that with the great majority of people three years are needed before the deeper strata of personal character begin to be purified and harmonized. I can only give my general impressions. After an absence of four months, during which I travelled round the world and saw the action of Subud on men and women of many races, I returned to England and began to observe the effect on several hundred people with whom I had previously worked. I am satisfied that there has been a general, sustained improvement both in the physical condition of these people and in their mutual relationships upon the reactional level. By this I mean that the frictions and misunderstandings between people of different ages, education, social class and attitude towards the responsibilities of life have certainly diminished and mutual trust has begun to develop. It is, however, true that the deeper forces - those described by Pak Subuh as the animal or motivating forces - have for the most part remained unchanged. It may well be that we shall have to wait for another two years before positive evidence of a fully harmonious development can be expected. Perhaps the most remarkable change that I have observed in people who have been following the Subud latihan for more than a year is the acquisition of confidence and self-reliance and the marked diminution of suggestibility and dependence upon others.

The third important addition made in this edition is a section on the experience of death. The reality of a continued existence after death cannot be doubted by those who have 'exercised for the dead'. It is also certain that the condition of man after death can vary from a state of bitter desolation and confusion to one of clarity and full consciousness. Modern man is afraid of death, but does not take it seriously. The almost universal indifference to the condition in which death is approached is appalling to anyone who has experienced the true state of affairs. In this respect the cleavage that has become universal between the medical profession and the priesthood is one of the most terrifying manifestations of present-day materialism. Children do not understand their duty towards parents who have died, husbands do not realize that dead wives need their help, nor do wives understand their connection with a dead husband. Most people probably believe that some kind of existence continues after death and the immense growth of the spiritualist movement is proof that many are deeply concerned with the problem of the after-life. But attempted communication through mediums is perhaps the most unsatisfactory way of probing into the unknown. A positive action is needed and one of the most amazing and awe-inspiring experiences of the Subud latihan is the direct evidence that is received of the true nature of the connection between the dead and the living. I have attempted to summarize this evidence in a new section of Chapter 8.

Life on this earth that does not take full account of death and its consequences is far more foolish than that of a man imprisoned for a short term who will not prepare for the time of his release. The prisoner will at least have hands and feet, eyes and ears when he re-enters the world of free men. The man who dies unprepared is lost in utter confusion and desolation from which he has no power to liberate himself. The full realization of the situation combined with the knowledge that those who survive have the power to help the dead would do perhaps more than anything to restore to mankind a sense of our spiritual obligations. It may well be that we have here the beginning of a new development that will have a profound influence on human life in the future.

Finally, a question that has been raised by several reviewers and many correspondents needs some explanation here. It has been suggested that since the Subud latihan requires nothing of us except the act of surrender to the Will of God and the acceptance of an action which, we believe, comes from the Holy Spirit, nothing remains for us to do except wait patiently for the results to come. Such an attitude, it is argued, leads to quietism and an unhealthy passivity in life. It is contrary to the principle that everything worth having must be paid for and, worst of all, it undermines the sense of human responsibility.

These arguments are based on the false premise that to surrender our will to the Supreme Will implies also surrender of our will in regard to our own inner and outer world. One of the great merits of Subud is the clear distinction that it makes between what man can and must do and what he cannot and should not attempt to do. Man can and must work both inwardly and outwardly, but he cannot understand the Power of God or the working of the Holy Spirit, and he should not attempt to rely upon his own strength to achieve his own purification. We receive a power that is not our own, but the exercise of the power remains our responsibility. This is made abundantly clear in Pak Subuh's own book Susila Budhi Dharma, but I have thought it necessary to add two sections to Chapter 8 in the hope that any doubts on the subject of human responsibility may be removed.

The objection that Subud is 'too easy' and does not demand effort, is a strange aberration to those who have practised it. It is easy to start, but to persist week after week and month after month is a real task for those on whom life presses hard. Patience is a great spiritual gift, and it is not easy to be patient when for long months nothing seems to happen. To be brought to see oneself in the light of Conscience and to experience repentance for all that one has done, and for all that one is, must be for everyone the hardest trial. But without repentance we cannot be saved. Those who seek to live according to their religious faith know well that sincere repentance is not achieved merely by wishing for it. The miracle of Subud is that all these things are made possible for us but to do them remains and must always remain a free act of our own will. No one should come to Subud who imagines that salvation can be bought cheaply; but for those who are willing to pay the price the reward is the growing awareness of being sustained in all trials by the Power of the Holy Spirit of God.

Coombe Springs
Kingston-upon-Thames
September 1958

FOREWORD

WORKING on this book, I have sometimes felt like a traveler who discourses on the affairs of a country in which he has spent seven days as a tourist. Subud is new to me as it is to all western countries. My personal contact is less than eighteen months old. I agreed to write *Concerning Subud* partly to correct many false impressions that have been formed from newspaper articles, and partly because the obligation to share with others what we our-selves value can only be discharged if we are ready to disclose our experiences. It is easy to shelter behind theories and what other people may have said or written, but this does not pay our own debt.

The obligation to make public one's own - often very private - reasons for following a certain course of action, has a salutary effect in making one answer the question "What really are my convictions in this matter?" I have set down my own conclusions, and some of the considerations which have led me to them; others, indeed the most cogent, cannot be expressed in words.

It is hard even to entertain the notion that a prodigious event has now occurred on the earth. The external evidence is meagre, but it has ever been so in the past. As Albert Schweitzer wrote in his *Quest of the Historical Jesus*, "What this something is, which shall bring new life and new regulative principles to coming centuries, we do not know. We can only dimly divine that it will be the mighty deed of some mighty original genius, whose truth and rightness will be proved by the fact that we, working at our poor half thing, will oppose him might and main - we who imagine that we long for nothing more eagerly than a genius powerful enough to open up with authority a new path for the world, seeing that we cannot succeed in moving it forward along the track which we have so laboriously prepared."

In my opinion, the true significance of Subud is not to be sought in its connection with special ways or methods of self-development, but in the possibility it opens to us all of witnessing a return of religious faith in the world. Since Subud has no distinctive dogma, and Pak Subuh himself repudiates any suggestion that Subud is either a substitute for religion or itself a new religion, it can be followed by those who seek to deepen their faith in Divine Providence irrespective of their specific beliefs or professions. When it is really understood that Subud does not undermine a single article of the Christian faith, but gives Christians a new understanding and a new force in their own worship, it can do for the Church what no amount of propaganda or pressure could ever do - that is, deliver it from the prevalent empty observances which come from the intellect or the emotions, and thereby restore the true worship of the soul. The same applies to Islam and the mosque, and to Judaism and the synagogue.

Men of all religions have succumbed to the spirit of the old Epoch, and have sought to worship God with mind, emotion and body - the same instruments that they use for the study of natural phenomena, or for doing their business - and the inevitable result has been the disappearance of true religion. When people come to understand not only that worship must come from the awakened soul and from the conscience of man but that means are to hand whereby the soul can indeed be awakened, we may expect changes so far-reaching and so rapid that within our present generation we may witness the birth of a new world.

My qualifications to write about Subud are meagre, but as no one is in a much better position, I have accepted the task. I owe very much to Pak Subuh - he has told me many things concerning himself and his work and about the future of Subud about which I cannot write. I hope, however, that by setting down my own impressions and interpretations and by abstaining. from giving incomplete quotations from unpublished material, I may have succeeded in making it plain that no one except myself is responsible for the opinions and conclusions expressed in this book. It would have been easier to write had the second volume of *The Dramatic Universe* been already published, because, although written before I met Subud, the conclusions reached in it are fully in accord with those in the last chapter of this book. The final revision has been delayed by the coming of Subud, which has brought with it so many new tasks and so many new problems that it seems impossible to accomplish all that needs to be done.

I believe that a great blessing has come to mankind, not through the mighty deed of some mighty original genius, but by the will of God, and because of this belief I have been prepared to set down my own experience for the benefit of others. I have written only what I believe to be right - not what I assert to be true. If in doing so I have offended any susceptibilities, I hope I may be forgiven.

INTRODUCTION

Modern man is a success. He can produce far more foodstuffs and more goods than his forefathers at a fraction of the cost in bodily and mental effort. His scientific and technical achievements have not only given him leisure, but provided endless means of enjoying it. He has accumulated so great a store of knowledge of the world in which he lives that he can never exhaust its possibilities. And still new knowledge and new techniques keep pouring in. Moreover, modern man has built up vast organizations for international co-operation, for health and social welfare, for the production and distribution of wealth and for the regulation of world economy - all of which should ensure him against the risks of war, revolution, slumps, epidemic diseases, and guarantee social justice and human progress on a scale and at a rate never known before.

Yet modern man is unhappy, and lives in fear rather than in hope as he looks towards the future. He is in this condition despite the optimism that is almost universally proclaimed by the leaders and thinkers of the greatest and most powerful nations of the earth. People no longer believe in their leaders, either political or philosophical or religious. They feel like the child in Hans Andersen's story, who, despite the acclamations of the courtiers, can see for himself that the Emperor, for all his new clothes, rides stark naked in his carriage.

Neither view of man can be denied. Man is successful, and still he is unhappy and afraid. Yet happiness and freedom from fear matter to him more than success. He might even sacrifice his prosperity if he were sure that he would be delivered from fear and unhappiness. But he is sure of nothing.

The cause of all this malaise is easy to trace, and many people are well aware of it. Man is outwardly rich and inwardly poor; strong in what he has and can do, weak in what he is and can feel. The outer world forces in human life have grown enormously; the inner world forces have not grown - perhaps they have even dwindled. Man's contacts with the visible, tangible world of matter and bodies have increased in every direction, his contact with the invisible, supra-sensible world of the spirit is less than in any previous period of history.

If the material world were reliable, and if man could obtain from it all that he needs or wants, then the loss of the spiritual world might be no great hardship. Materialists in recent decades have asserted that the greatest blessing that has ever been enjoyed by mankind is liberation from religious superstitions and naive beliefs in a spiritual or non-material world. They have said that, once set free from the illusions of religious belief, human progress need know no limits. A boundless horizon of technical achievements would make man Master, not only of the earth, but also of the whole Solar System, and perhaps even of the stars also. With limitless potentialities of new experiences and new powers, each generation could not only enjoy the present, but possess in their children the glorious future of mankind.

Today, these voices are no longer shouting their message from the housetops with the same assurance, or, if they are shouting, it is rather to keep up a courage that from year to year is undermined with doubt and disillusion. New voices are being heard that proclaim the downfall of mankind, the End of the Age. These prophets of doom are listened to, above all by the younger generation, that sees with bitterness that it has been brought into a world where success spells fear, and progress is the harbinger of misery.

There is only one way out, and that is the renewal of inward, spiritual vigour. Everyone knows this, and no one knows how it is to be achieved. Good counsel there is in plenty, but practical suggestions that will actually work are utterly lacking. Everything has been tried.

Religious revivals within and outside the Church have proved ephemeral. Universal education is a boomerang: the more we know, the more we want and cannot have. United nations and welfare states are losing their glamour. So far from

11

gaining an inner strength, man becomes from decade to decade more and more dependent upon external supports.

The majority of people can no longer eat what they wish, furnish their houses as they wish, use their leisure as they wish - but only as it is dictated to them by some form of propaganda. An American lady was standing in Piccadilly at the traffic lights, evidently in a state of helpless uncertainty. When asked what was the matter she replied, "In New York, we wait until the sign says WALK: then we walk. Here they don't tell you, so I don't know how to cross." Such is modem man in almost all that he does. However comical such situations may appear to others, they are not a laughing matter, for we are all in the same boat. Unless there is some extraordinary change, there will, within a century, be very few men and women left able to do anything unless they are urged to it by some effectual form of propaganda. Since freedom of judgment and the power of choice are the marks of a human being, we are bound to conclude that, within three or four generations, mankind will have ceased to be human.

Sheep at least do not think. At present some people still think a little and they are sometimes even appalled at the universal lack of initiative. Then they feel that for all our successes there is something terribly amiss with human affairs.

Such people turn to their religious leaders with the reproach: "You assure us that God is in His Heaven - tell us then why all is not right with the world." If there is no answer to this question, then man is thrown back upon his own resources, with the slender hope that if he can weather the threatening storm, a spiritual revival based upon a broad humanism may yet be promised.

But we all know too much of past history to have any confidence in such promises. Man has never yet lifted himself out of the mire by his own shoe-strings. The great renewals of the past have always come by the providential intervention of Sacred Beings who have been able by some incomprehensible power to re-establish faith, hope and love as the motive forces among their immediate followers, and these in their turn have been a leaven that has brought a new spiritual vigour to the multitudes. We cannot, at the present time, look for help in any power inferior to that of the Holy Spirit, the Lord and Giver of Life. But we are closed to the Spirit, just because the very qualities of faith, hope and love are lacking in us. Our hearts are hardened, and our ears are dull of hearing, and who shall deliver us?

Ten years ago, I gave a series of lectures in London, published afterwards as *The Crisis in Human Affairs*. Then I said, as now, that only Divine Intervention can save us. But then I added that we had not yet heard the voice of one crying in the wilderness. I received a letter from the late Dean Inge in which he wrote: "I agree with nearly all you write in your book - but I cannot promise a new revelation."

Now I am writing again after having seen many new things, and passed through prodigious experiences, to tell those who wish to hear that I believe that a new light has appeared on the horizon. In this light we can see the outlines of a great plan, or Purpose. There seems at last to be the possibility of a practical method or means whereby the hungry can be fed. It is all so new and so astonishing that it would in many ways have been better to wait for clearer proofs and a fuller understanding. But there is really no time to lose. If there is indeed a hope that very large numbers of people - in fact, all who ask for it - can receive the spiritual awakening that can begin a new life, then this hope should not be the treasured possession of a few.

I. THE NEW EPOCH

1. The Conscious Direction of Evolution

THANKS to the achievements of archaeology, anthropology, prehistory and several auxiliary sciences, it is now possible to reconstruct with some confidence the story of mankind for at least seven thousand years; and, with many gaps and uncertainties, for twenty-five thousand years, that is, back to the time when Aurignacian man first left evidence of a high culture. The human story goes back still further for at least half a million and perhaps one or two million years, but it is known only from a few hundred skeletons and a very limited range of stone implements that give us little idea how our remotest ancestors really lived. The whole story of life on the earth covers the hardly imaginable span of much more than five hundred million years. During this time prodigious changes have occurred in the dominant forms of life on earth and in the oceans.

It is no longer possible to account for the sequence of events on the supposition that no agency save blind chance has been at work, and that consciousness and a directive will were entirely lacking on the earth until men appeared. In Volume II of *The Dramatic Universe*, I endeavour to show how much simpler and more satisfying is the theory that the entire story, from its earliest beginnings, has been directed by Conscious Powers that have known how to make use of the uncertainty or freedom inherent in the operation of all the laws of nature, and bring about the progressive development of the living forms that were required at each successive stage of the evolution of the earth itself.

We cannot represent to ourselves the nature of such Conscious Powers, and we should certainly be wrong to picture them as individualized beings in any way resembling men - that is, having a body with limbs, organs, and perceiving by way of senses like ours. But it is no new thing for science to accept the reality of entities of which we can form no mental picture at all. Indeed, the recourse to 'unthinkables' has been one of the strangest developments of science since Planck introduced his mysterious quantum of action, and Einstein based his relativity theory on a Riemannian geometry that cannot be pictured by the senses or grasped by the mind.

We shall start then from the supposition that there always have been and still are Conscious Powers that regulate events upon the earth without violating the laws of nature. It may shock the susceptibilities of scientists - who are very touchy about supernatural entities that they have not themselves invented - if I call these Powers by the name of angels. I do not know who or what angels are, but for many years I have had no doubt that there are such beings, and that it is possible to be aware of their presence. I am equally sure that the angelic powers work within the framework of the natural laws of geometry, physics and biology.[1]

As we survey the past, with its vast time scale of cosmic, geophysical, palaeobotanical and palaeontological history flowing into the early prehistory and later history of man on the earth - we can observe one common and indeed universal phenomenon. This can be called 'progress by explosion'. History never has been continuous. The great changes in the families and genera populating the earth have come about suddenly, and have been followed by long periods of relative quiet. It would be out of place to review here all the evidence for the 'explosive theory of progress'. Indeed, the theory is not new, and has been adopted in many branches of science.

2. The Theory of Epochs

If we combine the Theory of Conscious Directive Power with the Theory of Explosive Progress we arrive at the notion of Creative Cycles. This is simply illustrated in the working of an

---

1   In Volume I of *The Dramatic Universe* I have shown that the 'natural' geometry of six dimensions has several degrees of freedom that allow full scope for a regulative consciousness even in the rigorous sciences of kinematics and electromagnetism.

internal combustion engine which alternates between phases of compression, explosion, expansion and renewal. The sudden explosions which occur in history can best be interpreted if we assume that the Angelic Powers direct natural energies for a certain time into a phase of concentration and compression that accumulates enough energy to make an explosion, the results of which then expand and grow until their force is exhausted. Explosions that occur without any system of regulation are inevitably destructive; and the incontrovertible fact that explosions have occurred over and over again in the history of the stars, of the earth, of life in general and of mankind in particular, and have resulted on the whole in progress towards higher levels of consciousness and a greater freedom, is the best evidence that the Conscious Directive Power of the angels has seldom been absent.

From the notion of Creative Cycles in general we come to that of the Epoch[1] in the life of man. By 'Epoch', I understand a period when all humanity is dominated by a certain creative attitude towards life. This I call the Master Idea of the Epoch. For example, the middle Neolithic Epoch, from about 11,000 to 8,000 years before the present, was marked by the idea of the *Earth Mother*. Until that time, nearly all the people of the earth were nomadic hunters or gatherers of fruit or sea foods. From 9000 B.C., serious agriculture began, and men first realized that it was possible to claim ownership of the land they worked and to accumulate material possessions. Since generation, i.e. birth-death-resurrection, is the essence of the agricultural cycle, men were able in that Epoch to receive the notion of birth-death resurrection as applicable to their spiritual life also. Thus the so-called 'fertility cults' were a real step forward in the spiritual development of man. The mutual need of the sexes in the spiritual life was an obvious fact to people who began to see the continuity of the family in their village settlements. The idea of the Earth Mother encouraged a matriarchal social

1   The Theory of Epochs is discussed in *The Crisis in Human Affairs*, Hodder & Stoughton, 1948.

system such as existed in the Neolithic Epoch.

The middle Neolithic Epoch began with an explosion that probably coincided with considerable disturbances of the earth's surface. It ended when a fresh change of climate led to the desiccation of the densely populated areas of Central Asia and North Africa, and it was succeeded by the Epoch of the Great Migrations that lasted from 6000 B.C. to the middle of the fourth millennium. This time the Master Idea was that of the *Search*; of which fragments remain to us in ancient myths and legends and epics in which man is depicted as searching for the secret of immortality. The instability of external conditions created a natural background for the realization that life on earth is precarious, and that salvation must be sought in the invisible world. It was during this Epoch that knowledge of the mysteries of life and death began to reach ordinary people from the hidden societies that were still in conscious relationship to the Angelic Powers.

The next Epoch coincides with the beginning of written history, and the appearance of priest-kings or semi-divine beings as rulers of the various nations of the earth. The founders of the earliest dynasties of Egypt, Mesopotamia, India, China and the Malay Archipelago were looked upon as half-god, half-human, and for this reason I have called the era that lasted from 3200 B.C. to 600 B.C. the Hemitheandric Epoch. Its Master Idea was that of the dependence of the common people upon the *Hero* for their welfare in this life and in the life beyond the grave. History proper begins about the same time, towards the end of the fourth millennium B.C., not only in the form of written accounts of dynasties and their achievements, but also in clearly decipherable records of events preserved in the ruins of ancient cities and monuments.

Mankind entered upon the Heroic Epoch with an immense heritage of languages, cultures, techniques and social organization built up over thousands of years.

Once again there was an explosion. During a brief period of a few centuries, extraordinary advances were made in every department of human life. The Hemitheandric Epoch ended about two thousand five hundred years ago with the unspoken discrediting of the notion of the Semi-divine Ruler. It was followed by the Megalanthropic Epoch, of which the Master Idea was that of *Individual Salvation*. We shall return to this later, since it leads directly to the theme of the present book.

3. *Divine Providence*

The theory of Epochs as a cycle of concentration, explosion and expansion requires that there should be a concentrating force that accumulates the energy needed for the explosion. This we ascribe to the Angelic Power, but the theory is not complete unless we go further and assume that the source of the Power itself is altogether beyond this visible world. An internal combustion engine is constructed so that compression comes from its own momentum, but the fuel that produces the explosion comes from beyond. Similarly, in human affairs the new impulse that comes with each succeeding Epoch reaches mankind from beyond the earth itself.

Arnold Toynbee in his great *Study of History* reaches virtually the same conclusion: that we are forced to believe that human history has been directed by a Merciful Power that comes from God and manifests through the Saints, Prophets and Founders of the great religions of the world. Without presuming to challenge Toynbee's deep historical insight, I would say that through fixing his attention upon Civilizations, which are but secondary human consequences, he has overlooked the significance of the Epochs that are the primary manifestations of Divine Providence in human affairs. Nevertheless, Toynbee strongly reinforces the argument for conscious intervention of the Angelic Powers by the distinction he makes between true and arrested civilizations. He estimates that there are now on earth many hundreds of human communities that were formerly under the direction of conscious leaders, but having at some time lost contact with them, failed to develop, and so have lingered on, preserving, in the form of customs now almost devoid of sense, traces of an ancient wisdom whose origin may go back before the beginning of written history five thousand years ago.

We are thus not leaving explored territory when we add to the theory of Conscious or Angelic Powers the principle of belief in Divine Providence. This belief cannot be called a 'theory', for it belongs to a realm that the mind of man is powerless to explore.

4. Times and Seasons

We know the history of the earth from a most fragmentary and unequal record, but even this is enough to convince us that from the remotest past, organic life on this planet has adapted itself to great changes of climate, has survived prodigious catastrophes and has gradually but surely moved forward to prepare a place for the coming of mankind. We cannot fail to be impressed by the timeliness of the explosions that have occurred as one form of life has given place to another. To an observer with ordinary human understanding watching the course of events, it would have seemed, time and again, that life on the earth must perish or degenerate into a miserable remnant of forms too insignificant to challenge the cataclysmic forces that disrupted the earth's surface and played havoc with its climate. And yet each time, by far-sighted manipulation of the genetic potentialities inherent in existing families and orders of plants and animals, the Angelic Powers brought forth new genera and species that could not only survive, but prosper in the new conditions.

When man appeared, our earth entered the great ice ages, when at times all life was threatened. According to some theories, such as that of Hoerbiger, there were other catastrophes caused by the destruction of a former satellite and the capture of our present moon. Whatever may be the truth of such theories, it is certain that during the million or more years of his existence on the earth, man has survived appalling changes of climate that required powers of adaptation quite different from those that saved the plants and animals of earlier ages.

I am sure that Saurat[1] is right in concluding that survival was achieved only by the timely direction of human energies into the sole channels which gave hope of safety-as for example in the Epoch of the Great Migrations away from Central Asia and North Africa when these regions dried up and fertile soil became desert sand.

Guidance in the outer life has always been based upon the renewal and strengthening of the inner life, and we can trace the gradual penetration of religious belief from the inner circle of those who had direct revelation of the Divine Purpose, into and through the masses of mankind. In the earliest periods, the superhuman beings who guided human destiny were very far removed from the savage hunting tribes that looked to them for help. They were disguised as magicians, and their rule was based upon dread of the powers that they were able to evoke. During the Neolithic ages - which probably included three distinct Epochs - there was a great transformation of social conditions, and the new stability and continuity of external life made it possible to impart to the masses forms of religious worship, of private and social morality, based upon belief in the presence in man of a mortal and an immortal part, each having a different destiny.

Many students of the early history of mankind are now convinced that from the earliest times man has believed in one God, the supreme power in the world, and that the crude animism observed in many savage tribes is not primitive at all, but the result of degeneration in the absence of guidance from conscious beings. If this conviction is justified, it must follow that there have always been teachers of mankind who have gradually prepared man to understand the true significance of our life here on earth. Such teachers could not have received their knowledge from any human source, for it is not given to man to know the Divine Purposes. It is in this sense that teachers or

---

1   cf. Denis Saurat, *Atlantis and the Giants*, Faber & Faber, 1957.

prophets are termed Messengers from God. The proof of their mission lies not so much in the loftiness and grandeur of their ethical teachings as in the timeliness and efficacy of their intervention. We do not attempt to teach metaphysics to infants, nor did any of the prophets throughout history attempt to teach men truths for which they were not ready. Each explosion that inaugurated a new Epoch corresponded exactly to what people were able to receive at that time.

We can take one or two examples to illustrate this theme. The city of Ur upon the river Tigris was already a great city at the beginning of the Hemitheandric Epoch in 3200 B.C. It flourished for more than two thousand years and was the centre of high cultures. When the Epoch was moving towards its period of degeneration about 1500 B.C., there was an exodus towards the west of which an account has been preserved in the book of Genesis, and of which hints can be found in old cuneiform writings of Chaldea. The leader of this exodus was a prophet whom we know by the name of Abraham. The story of Abraham is both true history and also an allegory of the power of faith. Through Abraham, the ancient monotheism was preserved from the universal degeneration that finally destroyed the hopes of the Epoch. The lesson for us in the story of Abraham consists in the extreme simplicity of his faith and his childish inability to understand the working of Divine Providence. Abraham's very simplicity was precisely what the age required, and it is to be contrasted with the marvellous scientific attainments of the Chaldean Magi and the Egyptian priests of the eighteenth dynasty who were his contemporaries. A similar contrast is to be found in the story of Moses, illustrated by his legendary contest with the Egyptian priests.

The Hebrew Torah is concerned to show how the prophets were endowed with a power from God that does not depend upon human science or human abilities. It insists upon the duty of preserving the ancient traditions, and calls for belief in the One God and in His providential ordering of human affairs. Nevertheless, if we were to attempt to transfer into our modern world the message and the example of Abraham, Isaac and Moses, we should see at once that they belong to a different Epoch from ours, and that the validity of their message is attested precisely by its combination of timeliness and timelessness. The fundamental truth that God will help those who turn to Him belongs to all Epochs, but the form of Abraham's message belongs only to the Epoch when men could readily believe that their prophets could 'speak with God', and were therefore ready to accept their autocratic leadership.

In order to grasp the significance of the Message brought to mankind by the early prophets of the next, that is the Megal-anthropic Epoch, we must picture to ourselves the almost universal wretchedness of the peoples of China, India, Assyria, Egypt and Greece at the beginning of the first millennium B.C. Some of the prophets, like Confucius and Solon, were mainly concerned with the social misfortunes of their nations, but the greatest of all were sent with a deeper message of hope for the afflicted. This was no less than the promise of *individual salvation* for every man and woman who was ready to pay the price. We are the descendants of a hundred generations who have lived with this promise, and we cannot readily picture the misery of those who believed themselves to be entirely dependent upon the Hemitheandros or Divine Ruler, and yet could see in their own kings and pharaohs only monsters of cruelty and oppression. The words of the prophet Isaiah, "Ho, everyone that thirsteth, come ye to the waters, and he that hath no money come ye, buy and eat" conveyed an entirely different meaning to the children of the Captivity to that which they would bear in our modern world. We cannot understand that the very hope of eternal life was destroyed for those who believed that only the Divine Ruler could ensure welfare beyond the grave and saw that their priests had become servants of the oppressor, extorting impossible payments for the performance of complicated rituals believed to be indispensable for the welfare of the dead. It was the hope of liberation from spiritual oppression that drew the Indian multitudes to Gautama

Buddha and the Israelites to their prophets.

Within five hundred years was fulfilled the sombre prophecy of Gautama Buddha that his Dharma would deteriorate and the Sangha break up into warring sects. All over the world the gospel of individual salvation had been misinterpreted and misapplied. And yet everywhere there was a sense of expectancy, made explicit by the Jewish belief in the coming of the Messiah and the neo-Buddhist doctrine of the Bodhisattva. The Greco-Roman world was disgusted with itself and its own moral failures. The Persian empire of the Seleucidae was sunk in impurity. India had lapsed grievously from the reforming zeal of King Asoka. Those who sought for purity, the Jains, the Pharisees, the Stoics, were discovering that purity could not be achieved by any human striving.

In response to a desperate human need, Almighty God sent into the world Jesus Christ, whose perfect purity is symbolized in His virgin birth. The message of Jesus was as simple and direct as those of His predecessors - by faith alone can man be purified in body and soul. Jesus was endowed with the power to work miracles because He was completely free from the impurities that in ordinary man obstruct the working of the spirit of God. What He taught He practised, and He proved by His death and resurrection that the pure spirit is indestructible. His message and His evidence gave an entirely new meaning to the doctrine of individual salvation, liberating it from all worldly considerations, placing the hope of mankind in the invisible world of the spirit, the Kingdom of Heaven.

Another six hundred years passed and once again the message had been distorted. The Kingdom of Heaven had become an earthly power, salvation was no longer sought in pure faith but in the toils of an enforced external discipline. Worst of all, the message of pure Love had been twisted into a mass of superstitions that even a true man of God like St. Benedict was powerless to overcome. The dark ages had descended upon the western world, and men were again living without hope and yet obsessed by the fear of damnation. A cardinal error had crept into Christian dogma - the belief that the celibate state is pleasing in the sight of God. Strangely enough, the repudiation of marriage and the belief that only ascetic practices can lead to liberation had taken possession also of the eastern stream of spirituality - especially in the forms of Buddhist monasticism and the solitary withdrawal from the world recommended by the Hindu Sannyasis and Yogis. Even those who still were seeking salvation did so in ways that can only in the rarest of cases lead to the complete human being that each man must become in order to enter into eternal life.

Once again a new message was needed, and it was brought by the Prophet Muhammad. He exemplifies the complete man who fulfils all his earthly obligations and yet whose will is wholly surrendered to the service of God. The message of Islam cannot be understood by those who have not realized something of the meaning of the complete man. Muhammad was rejected and denied by those who saw in his very completeness a lack of perfection, and who imagined that asceticism was a necessary mark of holiness. Nevertheless, the power of the Islamic revelation was so great that within two centuries a great belt of Islamic peoples stretched from end to end of the inhabited world from Morocco to the Malay Archipelago. By the tenth century A.D. Islam had become the greatest spiritual power in the world, but unfortunately Moslems, Christians and Jews, destined to unite and demonstrate to the world the invincible power of the Sacred Impulses of Faith, Love and Hope, succumbed to the disruptive forces of materiality, lust for power and fear. From the end of the first millennium the degeneration of the Divine Message of Individual Salvation into the cult of human self-sufficiency had become inevitable.

5. The Ages of Mankind

During recent centuries, the material forces in human life have gradually gained the mastery over the spiritual forces. Thus we have before us in the history of our own times the demonstration of the twofold nature of human potentialities.

The Master Idea of an Epoch is the highest expression of man's capacity for understanding his destiny at the spiritual age he has reached. Taking the rough estimate of twenty-five million years for the entire life-cycle of the genus *Homo* on this earth, the two or three thousand years occupied by an epoch is the equivalent of one week of our ordinary lives. Each week brings a new lesson that the child assimilates as best it may. So in each great epoch a new message is sent to mankind. Owing to the youth and inexperience of the human race, and to our inability to perceive what is beyond the senses, we make over and over again the mistake of interpreting the message in terms of this visible world and its passing values. If we look back to the messages of the past, we can see how this hazard has always been present, and how mankind has never learned to value the eternal above the temporal. But this must not be regarded as 'failure'. We do not expect children to acquire at one step the same learning as their teachers. Week by week new lessons are given - and mostly forgotten - but the process of education goes on.

If we look at history upon too small a scale of time, it looks like a story of material progress and social improvement, but of spiritual stagnation. Many people today say that although we have far more knowledge and far better social conditions than those of two or five or ten thousand years ago, we are just the same human beings; as selfish, as short-sighted and as discontented and full of fears as people have ever been. This diagnosis is valid only if we think of humanity as an already fully developed adult being. We must lift ourselves above the preoccupation with our immediate present. If we wish to understand human destiny, we must study it in relation to a much greater time-scale than that of the history of the past few centuries. When we are able to survey - even with our meagre knowledge - the history of mankind over half a million years and by applying the general law of cycles to make some estimate of future time, we begin to see a great and consistent pattern emerge from the confusion, and our faith is confirmed that

25

Divine Providence has never failed to intervene at moments of need to give mankind new lessons and new opportunities.

6. The Coming Epoch

The 'End of the Age' or the 'End of the World' are strange phrases that have been on men's lips for thousands of years. Sometimes they have conveyed a sense of urgency, as when the early Christians were awaiting, literally from day to day, the coming of the Lord, and thought it foolishness to be occupied with the affairs of a world that was soon to be destroyed or superseded by the Reign of Christ. Even when the 'latter days' belonged to some indefinite future, the belief remained that history would have an end, and utterly different conditions of existence would await those who 'endured to the end'. Belief in the Second Coming was not confined to the Christian churches. The Prophet Muhammad also foretold the future degeneration of religion and the coming of a time when men would give themselves up to the material or satanic forces. When certain signs were fulfilled, Jesus was to come again to the earth and separate the believers from the unbelievers, after which the final conflict of the good and evil powers was to come and end in victory for the righteous. According to some traditions, this victory was to be the signal for the immediate end of the world. According to others, it was to inaugurate the millennium, when the earth would be peopled only by the righteous, and only after a thousand years of earthly felicity was the last trumpet to sound. Since these prophecies are preserved only in the form of verbal traditions collected long after the death of Muhammad we cannot hope to reconstruct with any accuracy what he really foretold. Moslem eschatologists of the present time attach great importance to the *hadisat* - traditions of the Prophet - to the effect that in the latter days men would invent carriages that would run without horses and build houses as high as the hills. These and other portents of the End of the Age have now been accomplished, and I have met many Moslem learned men who believe that the Second Coming is imminent.

It is not possible to draw any definite conclusions from all the Jewish, Christian and Islamic traditions of a future 'End of the Age' beyond the most important of all - that is, that the future degeneration of religion was clearly foreseen by Those whose messages founded the Megalanthropic Epoch, and that they predicted a fresh intervention of Providence at the very time when the material or satanic powers would seem to be in the ascendant.

Again and again, men have believed that the latter days must have come and have expected the end of the world. The perennial disappointment of these expectations has led in modem times to a complete distrust of any literal eschatology, and those who look for the early Second Coming are generally regarded as dreamers or cranks.

Nevertheless, we have still with us the mysterious warning of Jesus that the Son of Man would come as a thief in the night and that few would recognize His coming. It is scarcely surprising that the world has failed to understand a message that was 'told in darkness' - that is, to people who had not yet been awakened to the spiritual realities.

2 A PERSONAL APPROACH

1 Gurdjieff

IN the present chapter, I shall give an account of the experiences that led me by the end of 1955 to expect that in the near future an important event connected with the New Epoch was to occur in England, and that this event would be heralded by the arrival from the East of a man endowed with special powers.

The story begins with my return to Gurdjieff in July 1948, after twenty-five years of separation. At our first meeting, he asked me to read three times the Ashiata Shiemash chapters of *All and Everything* - then still in manuscript form - adding that these were most important for me. Later, he returned to them often in conversation, and from his explanations it was clear that he regarded the awakening of Conscience in the soul of man as the only hope of achieving the 'Harmonious Development of Man' which was and is the aim of his system.

Here it is necessary to add a few remarks upon Gurdjieff himself. He was a real teacher-that is, one who brought an original lesson that he himself had learned from some higher source. Gurdjieff was no mere syncretist who weaves, more or less skillfully, into a single thread, strands taken from many older traditions. It is true that nine tenths of what he taught could be traced to known sources - Greek Orthodox monasticism, Sufi mysticism, the Kabbalistic cosmology, neo-platonism, the Areopagite, Pythagorean and Egyptian numerology, Buddhist and Lamaist psychology, to name only a few of the best known - and that his psychological exercises, including his remarkable rhythmic movements and ritual dances, were mostly of Moslem Dervish and Central Asiatic origin. But, when all that is derived from the past has been accounted for, there remains in Gurdjieff's system a residue of authentic innovation, not so much a specific doctrine as a new point of view that breaks with the past and sees beyond the disputes that have divided the religions of the world for the past thousand years. Gurdjieff points the way to the New Epoch, even though he himself may not have been permitted to enter the promised land.

Who and what Gurdjieff himself was, has always been an enigma. Those who were closest to him were the most certain that they had never understood him. I myself met him for the first time in 1920 at Kuru Tcheshme, the palace of Prince Sabaheddin of Turkey on the Bosphorus. Later I spent a short time at his Institute at Fontainebleau in France. I saw much of him at the end of his life, and was with him for the last time a few days before he died. I have read his unpublished autobiographies - for there are more than one - and I have heard stories of his early life from members of his family, and of the period before 1920 from friends who had known him since the early days of this century. Each person gives a different account of him. He is already a legendary figure - the hero or villain of fantastic stories connected with the Dalai Lama, Stalin, the Emperor Nicholas II, Hitler and George Bernard Shaw. Some say he was admitted to a hidden brotherhood in Central Asia, whose secrets he stole in order to set himself up as a teacher in the West. I am sure that all such tales are wide of the mark. The mystery of Gurdjieff was much deeper than sham occultism or political intrigue. He made upon me the impression of an exile from another world who must always be a stranger in any company. There is undoubtedly much autobiography in *Beelzebub's Tales to his Grandson*, and when asked outright if Beelzebub were a portrait of himself, Gurdjieff often hinted at an affirmative reply.

I am not concerned here to make an assessment of Gurdjieff or his teaching, but only to suggest that he must have foreseen the coming of Subud and even drew in Ashiata Shiemash a picture of the messenger who was to come in our time.[1] Apart from the predictions made in his writings, Gurdjieff in the last

---

1   cf. *All and Everything*, pp. 347-go. Gurdjieff explained that these chapters are prophetic and that Ashiata Shiemash, the Prophet of Conscience, was still to come.

months of his life referred many times to his own imminent departure from this world and to the coming of another who would complete the work that he had started. He even said once that the one who was to come "is already preparing himself a long way from here" (i.e. from Paris). At another time, in 1949, he gave a clear indication that his pupils should seek for links with the islands of the Malay Archipelago. I must say that I did not at the time believe that Gurdjieff was soon to die or that the coming of the promised Teacher would occur in my own lifetime.

It will, therefore, be understood that after Gurdjieff's death in 1949, many of his followers[1] awaited the coming of another teacher who would take up the work that Gurdjieff had left unfinished.

2. Alice Bailey and the Arcane School

Gurdjieff was by no means the only writer to predict the imminent appearance on earth of a Messenger who was to renew the hope of mankind. One of the chief exponents of the doctrine of a spiritual hierarchy now working in the world to prepare for the second Coming of Christ was Alice Bailey, Founder of the Arcane School. I had hoped to meet Mrs. Bailey when I went to New York with Gurdjieff in January 1949, but unfortunately she was then near the end of her earthly life, and I know her only through her friends and her writings.

In one of her later books, *The Reappearance of the Christ*, published in 1948, Alice Bailey declared boldly that throughout the world preparations were being made for the Second Coming of Christ who would appear, not alone, but with helpers with different degrees of spiritual power. She starts with the doctrine of Avatars which she interprets to mean Messengers "coming down with the approval of the higher source from which they come and with benefit to the place at which they arrive".

The prediction is made in very general terms: "Humanity in all lands today awaits the Coming One - no matter by what

---

1   cf. Kenneth Walker's *Venture with Ideas*, the last pages.

name they may call Him. The Christ is sensed as on His way. The second coming is imminent and, from the lips of disciples, mystics, aspirants, spiritually-minded people and enlightened men and women, the cry goes up, 'Let light and love and power and death fulfil the purpose of the Coming One'. These words are a demand, a consecration, a sacrifice, a statement of belief and a challenge to the Avatar, the Christ, who waits in His high place until the demand is adequate and the cry clear enough to warrant His appearance.

"One thing it is most necessary to have in mind. It is not for us to set the date for the appearing of the Christ or to expect any spectacular aid or curious phenomena. If our work is rightly done, He will come at the set and appointed time. How, where or when He will come is none of our concern. Our work is to do our utmost and on as large a scale as possible to bring about right human relations, for His coming depends upon our work."[1]

Although the general conceptions set out in Mrs. Bailey's book are not very original and have much in common with the earlier prophecies of the founder of the Theosophical Society, Helena Blavatsky, there are suggestions of a more specific insight into the nature of the task to be accomplished. Thus she writes: "We can freely aid in the reconstruction work which the Christ proposes, if we will familiarize ourselves and all men whom we can contact with the following facts:

"1. That the reappearance of Christ is imminent.

"2. That the Christ, immanent in every human heart, can be evoked in recognition of His appearance.

"3. That the circumstances of His return are only symbolically related in the world Scriptures; this may produce a vital change in the preconceived ideas of humanity." She adds "a world at peace" as a fourth requirement. Mrs. Bailey further recognizes that the mind of man must of necessity be unreceptive to the new message. "It is possible surely that the ancient

---

1   Alice Bailey, *The Reappearance of the Christ*, Lucis Press, 1948, p. 188. There are also references to the Second Coming in her Autobiography.

truism that 'the mind is the slayer of the real' may be fundamentally true where the mass of humanity is concerned and that the purely intellectual approach (which rejects the vision and refuses to accept the unprovable) may be far more at fault than the anticipation of the Knowers of God and the expectant multitude."[1]

The central theme of Alice Bailey's writings is the presence on earth of a Hierarchy of conscious beings responsible for guiding human destiny and, at the present time, of preparing the coming New Age. At the head of this Hierarchy is Jesus Christ, but Alice Bailey also refers to a mysterious Power, the Avatar of Synthesis, incarnated for the first time on earth, with the task of bringing about the unification of humanity.

She affirms that, "As a result of Christ's decision and His 'spiritual fusion' with the Will of God, The Avatar of Synthesis has become for the time being His close Associate. This is an event of supreme and planetary importance." She describes the coming task as comprising three parts, functions or activities:

"*(a)* The production of a human synthesis or unity which will lead to a universal recognition of the *one humanity*, brought about through right human relations.

" *(b)* The establishing of right relations with the subhuman kingdoms in nature, leading to the universal recognition that there is *One World*.

"*(c)* The anchoring of the Kingdom of God, the spiritual Hierarchy of our planet, in open expression on Earth, thus leading to the universal recognition that the *sons of men are one*."[2]

The Avatar of Synthesis seems to be a symbolical representative of Subud in much the same way as Gurdjieff's Ashiata Shiemash. Alice Bailey refers also to a new Group of World Servers whose functions seem much akin to the Brotherhood Heechtvori of Gurdjieff.

3. General Expectancy in the World

If we should not attach too much importance to the

---

1   Ibid. pp. 58-g.
2   Ibid. p, 78.

predictions of occultists and kabbalists and astrologers, we cannot disregard the universal expectancy of some great event that is to change the course of history and save mankind from what otherwise would seem inevitable destruction. The expectancy of an Event has been particularly strong throughout Asia, South America and Northern Africa, but it has not been absent in Europe and the western seaboard of North and South America. That there really is a general sense of expectancy can be tested if we compare the present state of the world with that of thirty to forty years ago when the peoples of East and West emerged from the Great War hoping that their problems had finally been solved and that a tranquil, prosperous future awaited them. It seemed then that the future would be like the past - but exempt from the fears and injustices that had marred the social life of the nineteenth century. Even when these hopes were shattered by revolutions, economic crises and war, it still seemed as if a solution might be found. But by 1948 the threat of a disastrous third world war had cast its shadow over all people, and the great majority could see no way of escape.

Indeed, according to all precedent, war should have come during the tense years from 1948 to 1957. The piling up of weapons of destruction has been on a more alarming scale than ever before in history: the statesmen of the world have made the same grievous mistakes that they have always made; the perennial suspicions among allies have been no less rife than they have always been since Thucydides wrote, and yet war did not come. Only arrogance near to madness could lead any nation or any statesman to claim credit for the continuance of a precarious peace. Much the same could be written of threatening economic disasters, of food and population crises and of racial conflicts. The world has been in a terribly disturbed state, and the simple truth is that human affairs have gone far better than anyone had the right to expect. We are too close to events to see how strange they are, but if we view them from the perspective of all human existence on the earth - as we have attempted to do in the first chapter - we are bound to recognize in our present time the intervention of a Higher Power that is protecting mankind from the worst consequences of its own folly and unbelief.

Evidence of the real presence of a new force in the world can be found in the very great numbers of people - hundreds of thousands in each of the greater nations of the world -who have been moved to search for a way of salvation that they cannot find by conforming to the precepts and rituals of organized religious bodies. The revolt against Christendom inaugurated by Kierkegaard in 1850 was profoundly religious, and so also is the revolt against the churches that is so widespread in all countries today. It is very far from the indifference that emptied synagogues, churches and mosques in the years between the two wars. The best way to test for oneself the truth of the assertion that a new force is working in the world is to travel in many countries and mix with many people; one then sees that the phenomenon is not confined to any one continent, or race or creed, and that it is all the more significant in that for the most part people are unaware that their experience is shared by millions of others. There is a general thirst for a new life, combined with the belief that it must be possible to find it.

When we bring together the various threads, we can see that the human race is about to enter a new Epoch, and that people are looking for an inward change rather than for some reform of the outer life. The clearest indication of the form this change will take comes from Gurdjieff - it will be the awakening of the sacred impulse of *conscience*, made possible by the appearance of a man himself awakened and capable of transmitting the contact to others. Concerning the change of Epoch, I will quote what I wrote in 1947:

" ...our responsibility towards ourselves, towards other people, and towards those things which are beyond our personal concern, is that we should seek a way to ensure that our ears shall not be closed and that our eyes shall be able to see when the time comes. This is the aim of the psychokinetic attitude to man, the opening of possibilities in our essence, the opening of the inward eye and of the inward ear, which are able to perceive indications coming from a different level. If we have seen the character of the situation which confronts the world, and if we look ahead over the next period, we see that we entirely depend upon help of a very different kind from any that we can see around us today. The essential difference between an Epoch and Civilizations is that the former originates in Revelation from beyond humanity, while the latter are the work of schools within humanity itself. If I am right in the conclusion that we are witnessing the end of an Epoch and not the transition from one form of Civilization to another, we must place the hope of the world in a fresh Revelation of the Divine Purpose of Mankind and prepare ourselves to be ready to receive it."[1]

The prediction embodied in this passage was to be fulfilled within ten years - much sooner than I myself dared to expect.

4. Personal Experiences

In the last section, I tried to show that there have been many indications that we are about to witness positive manifestations of the Master Idea of the New Epoch, as distinct from the break-up of the Old Epoch that dates back to 1848. No one will be convinced by these indications unless he himself has felt the urge to search for a new way of life. Those who have found this are under an obligation to show the way to those who are still searching, and it is in fulfilment of this obligation that this book has been written. Since the content cannot be conveyed by words, and the outer form has no importance, the best I can do is to describe as well as I can my own experience before and since meeting with Subud.

It was Gurdjieff who first taught me and many others to look for the awakening of a higher consciousness, or higher centres, that cannot be reached by way of thought. It was he also who led us to expect the advent of a man who would hold the key to this awakening. In conversations during the last weeks of his life, Gurdjieff impressed upon me personally my obliga-

---

1   cf. *Crisis in Human Affairs*, pp. 230-1.

tion in connection with these future events. He told me certain things that have in part been fulfilled - others, including the most important, are still to come. The time has not yet arrived when these predictions can be disclosed.

When Gurdjieff died, he left behind him numerous groups of followers that he had made no attempt to weld into a single body. On the contrary, he seemed to have entrusted each group with different tasks to be accomplished independently. As far as I was concerned, it was clear that my duty was towards several hundred pupils who had gathered round me at Coombe Springs, the headquarters of the Institute for the Comparative Study of History, Philosophy and the Sciences, that I had founded in 1946 with the aim of studying "the factors making for development and retrogression in man". The lectures and courses given at the Institute were based upon Gurdjieff's system for the Harmonious Development of Man. Numerous study groups were organized. These, by 1957, had more than five hundred members in London, the provinces and abroad, who were being trained on the basis of Gurdjieff's psychological and physical exercises.

5. Emin Chikhou

I must here mention that throughout my life I have received indications in the form of an inner voice that I recognized as not coming from my ordinary self. Long experience has taught me that whenever I have neglected these indications I have run into trouble, and when I have trusted them I have been shown very clearly the way that I should go. It was in response to such an indication that in the autumn of 1953 I left for a time my work in England and travelled in South West Asia, where my knowledge of the languages of these countries enabled me to meet people not usually encountered by European visitors.

This journey was for me an extraordinary experience, for it brought into the open all the vague intimations of a coming event that I had previously placed in the distant future, long after my own death. I met members of the Nakshibendi Order of Dervishes, and spent three weeks with one of their brotherhoods whose headquarters is in Damascus. I found another group in an Anatolian village near the Euphrates, and yet another in Mosul on the Tigris. All these dervishes or Sufis were convinced that the End of the Age was imminent and urged me to prepare myself for the arrival of the Prophet of the Latter Days, who they assured me was already living on the earth and had sent news of his presence to the heads of the brotherhood. While in Damascus I met almost daily the Sheikh of the brotherhood, Emin Bey Chikhou, who spent most of his time endeavouring to prove to me from the Qur'an and the Hadisat that the signs of the end of the age were now being fulfilled. All this did not surprise me, for I was aware that Arabs are addicted to such speculations. I was, however, astonished when he assured me that I, John Bennett, was destined to be an opener of the way for Western people, and that when the chosen one arrived I was to stand beside him and be one of the witnesses to the authenticity of his mission.

6. Sheikh Abdullah Dagestani

I must say that Emin Bey's arguments did not convince me, and when I returned to England I said very little about this part of my journey. Two years later, however, I again received an indication: this time that I should go to Persia, and again I met several remarkable men, among others a Sheikh Abdullah Dagestani, whom I found under strange circumstances.

The whole story is worth recounting, for it is linked with many later events connected with Subud. On my journey to Persia by way of Damascus and Baghdad, I received a message through a complete stranger I met in Nicosia that I should visit in Damascus a certain Sheikh Abdullah al Dagestani. I was given no address, but told that I should ask for a barber called Ali the Turk whose shop was opposite the Tomb of Sheikh Muhyiddin ibn Arabi. I decided I could not go, as my time-table did not allow a stay in Damascus. However, the transport over the desert was delayed, and I found myself with a free evening.

I went up to the Kurdish quarter of Damascus which I know fairly well, and found Ali's shop, only to learn that he had been taken ill to hospital, and no one knew where I could find him. No one I asked had heard of Sheikh Abdullah. This did not surprise me, for in that quarter they are not very forthcoming to strangers.

Before returning to the city I went through the Mosque down into the crypt, where the Tomb of the Saint is visited by pilgrims. On an impulse, I prayed before the tomb, and felt once again the presence of a living force that I had experienced on my previous visits. When I came out of the Mosque again, I ran into an old hadji who had been my guide on an earlier visit, when I went up to Arbaein, a place of pilgrimage for Muslims as the legendary site of Cain's killing of Abel. There, according to tradition, the rocks were about to fall on him to avenge the fratricide, and were stayed by the Archangel Gabriel since it was the Will of God that Cain should live and beget children. This time the same guide was waiting as if expecting me, and asked where I wanted to go. When I told him, he said that he knew the Sheikh well and would take me to his house. Being sunset, he would probably be in a tiny mosque built for his private prayer beside his house. However, when we arrived Sheikh Abdullah was waiting for me on the roof of his house. I was relieved to find that he spoke excellent Turkish, and after the usual greetings he began to speak to me about myself.

Sheikh Abdullah is a true saint in whom one feels an immediate complete trust. With him there were no lengthy arguments or quotations from the scriptures. He simply said to me, "I was expecting you. Last night an angel appeared to me and told me to give three messages to a stranger who would come to my house." The first two messages were clear and unmistakable answers to very important questions that were troubling me about my work in England, and about which the Sheikh could not possibly have known by any ordinary means. They convinced me that he must have powers of a kind that I had already seen in Gurdjieff and one or two others, and prepared me to take very seriously anything that he might say.

We were sitting in the evening on the open roof of a house on the hills overlooking the ancient city. The Sheikh was a man of over seventy, dressed entirely in white, with a turban and white beard but with a youthful complexion and a steady humorous eye. One could scarcely imagine a setting more appropriate to the transmission of a solemn message, and just as the sun was setting he began to speak to me of the manifestation of the power of God in the world. The Old Age was dominated by satanic influences, but the time had come when all was to be changed. He spoke of the man who was soon to appear and through whom the power was to be manifested. It would not be right for me to set down here all that he actually told me, for the event is not yet complete. My only reason for telling the story is that it was an important factor in my subsequent decisions.

After saying that someone would come from the East, Abdullah startled me by telling me that not only was I chosen by God to be an immediate helper of this 'someone', but that he would come to England and even live in my house. He added that when I returned to England I should prepare a place for him, and assured me that henceforward I would be guided and protected in all my doings. It is hard to explain why I found myself taking seriously such a fantastic story and why, on my return to England, I began, without explaining my reasons, to prepare Coombe Springs to receive an extraordinary visitor.

7. Hadji Ahmad al Tabrizi

Kerind in Northern Persia is an ancient village set in a mountain gorge of uncommon beauty. For more than a thousand years the villagers have worked in steel and copper. It is a blessed place where there are no newspapers or radio and where a hundred yards from the main street a foreigner will draw crowds of amazed onlookers.

Through Kerind village gush innumerable streams, and waterfalls are everywhere. Above the village the valley opens and Kurdish herdsmen come down from the mountains with their flocks. Living in a hut beside the tomb of a forgotten Moslem saint, I met an old Dervish, Hadji Ahmad al Tabrizi, whose North Persian Turki dialect was reasonably easy to understand. He has a place in this story because, looking back three years, I see him as a link between Gurdjieff and Subud. Ahmad Tabrizi is a man whose inward peace and complete surrender to the Will of God cannot be doubted by anyone who meets him - even if they cannot understand what he says. I had a long talk with him arising from my question: "What makes the true dervish?" He replied:

"I can only speak from my experience. I have never belonged to any brotherhood, but have wandered over the world from the Gobi to the Arabian Desert. Wherever I have found someone from whom I could learn, I have stayed with him as long as was necessary, then I resumed my wanderings. This continued for forty years and then I found that I would not receive the teaching I needed from anyone except God. For the last ten years I have lived where I happened to be, when I was no longer wanted I went away. Now I am in this place and I would like to stay to the end of my life, but if it is not the Will of God I shall move again. Wherever I am, I have peace and prosperity for I can supply all my needs with my own hands. I am now more than seventy years old, but I could walk ten thousand parasangs to visit Kerbela again or Mecca, if it should be the Will of God.

"You ask me the secret of the true dervish. I say that it is surrender to the Will of God. Some people believe that it is good to enter a brotherhood such as the Djellalis or the Kadiris. Even in these present days there are good brotherhoods devoted to God's Will and whose dervishes call constantly upon His name. But we do not really need such practices, for His angels will protect us in everything. The man who does not surrender to God's Will becomes inevitably the slave of this world and cannot escape from it even if he unceasingly calls upon the name of God."

These simple statements, made as if they were self-evident, produced a strong impression on me. I could see for myself that I was sitting with a man in whom Conscience was awakened, and who lived by his conscience at every moment of the day. I had met one other such old dervish, a Mevlevi, Farhad Dede in Aleppo. Though both these old men had never been in contact with Europeans, I felt that if I could bring them to England they would be witnesses to many of the powers that enter man when his personal self-will is surrendered. Moreover, I realized that both would cheerfully have faced the complete disruption of their peaceful existence and would have accepted my invitation, had they felt that in doing so they would be serving the Will of God. When I left Hadji Ahmad Tabrizi, I knew that I had received a lesson that I must never forget. All my life I had tried to 'do' too much, and was still the slave of my own self-will. If I was to make a step forward, I must find the way to leave my self-will behind. In some way Hadji Ahmad had reinforced the feeling that when I returned to England many things would begin to change.

8. Intimations from the Far East

During 1956, I first began to receive indications that a new force had appeared in the Far East. Letters from Japan referred to a 'Master' whose pupils were following Gurdjieff's teaching without having heard of Gurdjieff.

A friend in Hong Kong wrote guardedly about a strange invitation to take part in 'spiritual exercises' which he did not understand. Later another old friend in Cyprus told me that he had made contact with an English Moslem, Husein Rofé, who had spent some years in Indonesia and claimed to be able to transmit a contact with a great Force, and who seemed to be familiar with the works of Ouspensky and Gurdjieff. Several references to Indonesia reminded me of Gurdjieff's hint that we should keep in touch with the Dutch Indies. Finally, in September 1956, I met Rofé himself, and was confronted with the question whether or not his Master or Guide, Muhammad

Subuh, was the one whose coming Gurdjieff and others had prophesied.

In November that year I went to America to see Madame Ouspensky, the widow of P. D. Ouspensky, who is recognized by the pupils of Gurdjieff throughout the world as the wisest counsellor and friend of all those who follow his system. I told her much of what I have written in this chapter and asked her advice. She said, "Ever since Mr. Gurdjieff went, I have been expecting someone to come - now seven years have passed, and no one has come. Whether he will come during my life or not, I do not know. But we must try everything and see for ourselves. If you wish to try this, why not do so? I advise you to keep it to yourself and a few friends with long experience."

On my return to England, I joined with eleven other former pupils of Ouspensky and Gurdjieff who had previously asked Rofé to give them the contact of which he had spoken. It was clear to me from the start that we had met with something very different from anything we had known before. After a few weeks some of us met to talk over our experiences, and we all agreed that they corresponded to the 'awakening of Conscience' that Gurdjieff had described.

In March 1957 I went again to America and met there both Madame Ouspensky and Madame de Salzmann, who is the recognized leader of the Gurdjieff groups in France, England and America. When I had recounted my experiences and impressions, both ladies agreed that it was necessary to investigate Subud thoroughly. I said that we had learned that Pak Subuh himself would come to Europe if he was invited. It was agreed that we should send the invitation and withhold judgment until we had met him.

Madame Ouspensky asked me how I would recognize a real teacher. I said that I had met many unusual men, but none so extraordinary as Gurdjieff. I did not think I could be deceived if I met a man who might have strange powers but not real Being. Madame Ouspensky said, "That is perhaps true. But you cannot rely on yourself. My advice to you is to *pray*. Only prayer will help before such a question."

The stage was set and the invitation was sent. Pak Subuh with his wife and three Indonesian helpers arrived in London on the 22nd May, 1957. I met him at the airport, having received permission to go through to Immigration. I found him sitting quietly on a chair waiting for the others to come through. In the midst of the usual tumult of arrival, I was impressed by two things: one was the *ordinariness* of his appearance, and the other was the sense of complete calm and detachment which not only came from him but entered into me also as soon as I saw him.

From the first evening of his arrival, I saw and learned many things that convinced me personally that I was on the right path. My conviction was not shared by others who are leaders of Gurdjieff's groups, and to whom it appeared that Subud was something new to be entered only at the price of breaking away from Gurdjieff. Since respect for the beliefs of others is common ground for any sane attitude towards life on this earth, I do not question the decision of those who have elected to follow strictly in the path traced by Gurdjieff and his principal exponents, P. D. Ouspensky and Maurice Nicoll. I have given my own reasons for believing that the coming of Subud was foreseen and foretold by Gurdjieff. These reasons are necessarily subjective, and cannot be valid for another person who has not passed through the same experiences.

In any case it is quite clear that Subud was never intended to be transmitted only to Gurdjieff's followers. Pak Subuh himself says that it is not tied to any religion or method. For Christians, Subud can be a means - indeed a miraculous means - for deepening their Christian faith and enabling them to see the literal truth of words that are too often uttered without inward conviction. The same is true for Jews and Moslems as well as for the followers of the Eastern religions. For those who follow special ways and systems, such as that of Gurdjieff, that seek the awakening of the higher consciousness latent in man, Subud seems to me to offer a most powerful instrument for achieving what they know to be necessary but find in practice to be beyond their powers. The value of prior preparation has been made abundantly clear to me after nearly two years' experience of Subud. Eighty per cent of those who came to Subud with previous training in Gurdjieff's system have persisted through the initial difficulties and still follow the latihan. Less than 40 per cent of those without such preparation can see the necessity for passing through the difficult and painful process of self-observation and the abandonment of the illusions of one's own importance and even of one's own existence. I can say for myself that not only has my Christian faith been strengthened, but I have found it possible to achieve much of what I had for many years striven for through Gurdjieff's method. Moreover, I have *seen* for myself - what I have always *believed* to be true - that the Christian faith is in no way incompatible with the beliefs of Judaism and Islam. The more one sees, the more one understands that all the great religions are deeply and fundamentally true. It is not only their ethics or their belief in a higher human destiny, or even the belief in God, that is true, but the very dogmas that appear to be in contradiction with one another - each is true, and true, moreover, literally and with no need for gloss or compromise.

It is the growing realization of the unity of the Divine Purpose throughout all human history that is for me the strongest evidence that Subud is also a manifestation of the Divine Purpose, and has been sent to the world at a time when help is most needed.

3. THE COMING OF SUBUD

1. Birth and Early Years of Muhammad Subuh[1]

THE events recounted in this chapter up to 1956 are known to me only through what Pak Subuh has told me of his own experiences, and what we have heard from his Indonesian followers. I cannot reproduce all that we have been told, for Pak Subuh wishes that 'hearsay evidence' should be as far as possible excluded from this account. I am obliged therefore to confine myself almost solely to those events which, having been witnessed by others than Pak Subuh, could, in principle at least, be verified independently. The deep impression made upon those to whom Pak Subuh has spoken of his own personal experiences is necessarily lost by this restriction, but it seems right that some account should be given of the manner in which Subud came into the world. Of course, this can only be known 'externally', that is, on the level of our sense experience which belongs to the lowest or material world. What we call 'facts' are really only shadows of shadows - but since they are all that we see, they are all that we can describe. My facts are meagre, but they may help the reader to form his own picture.

Though of noble descent, Pak Subuh's parents were small farmers in Kedung Djati near Semarang, a town in Middle Java. He was born on 22nd June, 1901, and it is recorded that many volcanoes erupted and earth tremors were observed in Java in those days. According to custom, his father chose his name and called him Sukarno.

The child fell sick and for several days could not take food. His death seemed inevitable and the women of the house

---

1   SUBUH, the personal name, comes from an Arabic word meaning sunrise or dawn. SUBUD, the name given to the activity as a whole is the contraction of three Sanskrit words explained in Chapter VI. To avoid confusion, I shall use the prefix PAK which means father, a common Indonesian term for respected elderly gentlemen, to designate the man Muhammad Subuh.

were wailing their laments, when an old man passing by asked the reason, and on being told that a child was dying, asked his name. He said that the name was wrongly chosen and that he should be called Muhammad Subuh. His father accordingly changed his name and, from that moment, the child began to take food and grew up strong and healthy.

His mother being occupied with her younger children, his upbringing was mostly left to his grandmother. As soon as he could speak, the child gave proof of clairvoyant power, discovering lost objects and foretelling events that were to occur to people he met. When asked by a journalist to give an example, Pak Subuh said that when less than three years old, his grandmother had taken him to a betrothal ceremony. He declared that the couple, who had not yet seen one another, were incompatible and would separate within a year. When his prediction was duly fulfilled, his grandmother refused to take him to any more betrothals. Apart from such external manifestations, the child frequently received inner indications about his life and behaviour. He found especially that when he was in the company of other children who told lies to hide their faults and misdeeds, he could not bring himself to imitate them. He even tried, as an experiment, to see if he could speak falsely and found that his voice always refused to make the required sounds.

When about sixteen years of age, Subuh received clear and repeated indications that he was to die on reaching the age of thirty-two. Since his experience had led him to accept such indications as completely reliable, Muhammad Subuh decided to leave school and search for the reason for his strange fate. In Java, there were many teachers or Gurus. There were Christian priests, Catholic and Protestant, orthodox Moslem Ulema, as well as Sufi murshids. There were also Chinese Taoists and Buddhist monks, Hindus, and ancient Javanese communities that had preserved traditions of the Far Eastern archipelago that probably go back more than five thousand years. Muhammad Subuh went from one to another of these teachers. One of these was Sheikh Abdurrahman of the same Nakshibendi order of dervishes as Sheikh Abdullah Dagestani. This is now the most flourishing of all the Sufi orders, with members throughout the Moslem world. Muhammad Subuh soon observed that the Sheikh would not impart to him the same teaching that he was giving to other pupils, and was sad to feel that he was neglected. When he asked the reason, Sheikh Abdurrahman replied, "You are not of our kin - it is not meet that I should teach you." Muhammad Subuh wondered what this could mean, and even asked himself if he was of the kin of Satan that no one should wish to teach him. Another time, when he was only twenty years old, he visited an old woman in East Java who was famous for her wisdom and spiritual gifts, and to whom many of the Ulema and learned men came for teaching. When he entered the room, where she sat surrounded by her pupils, she astonished them all by rising, paying reverence to him, and asking him to occupy her place.

Again and again, he found that the teachers he went to refused to answer his questions and declared that he was not of the same stuff as they. When pressed, they told him that his answers would never come from man, but by direct Revelation from God. None of this satisfied Muhammad Subuh, for his chief wish was to be an ordinary man and to live an ordinary life.

Realizing finally that his quest was fruitless, Muhammad Subuh decided that his right course was to undertake and fulfil the normal duties of man on this earth - that is, to take care of his parents, to marry and beget children, to earn his living and to take his place as a member of the society to which he belonged. He became a book-keeper and worked for fourteen years, first in commerce and later in local government service as assistant to the treasurer of the town of Semarang. In speaking of his years as a householder, Pak Subuh has described the success of the various undertakings he served. In his last post, he saw within two years a municipality that had always been insolvent, balance its budget and find money for various under-takings needed for the people's welfare.

2. *The Beginning of the* Latihan

In Muhammad Subuh's twenty-fourth year, he had the first of a series of remarkable experiences that led to his final understanding of his mission in life. One night in the summer of 1925, he was walking in the open under a moonless sky, when he saw high above his head a ball of brilliant light that seemed brighter than the noonday sun. While he was wondering about the meaning of this apparition, the light itself descended and entered him through the crown of his head, filling his body with radiance. The vibrations produced in his body and feelings by this experience were the first intimation of the working of the spiritual exercises which later were to be known by the name of Subud. That the apparition of the ball of light was not a subjective hallucination peculiar to himself is indicated by the fact that many friends in the town and even many miles away also saw it and came the next morning to his house to enquire what had happened. On subsequent occasions, others, especially his mother, witnessed the same phenomena as himself and often could verify and amplify his own descriptions.

For nearly three years, such experiences were a nightly occurrence, so that he scarcely slept by night, and yet he found the strength to fulfil his life obligations by day. He neither sought nor welcomed the inner working, chiefly because he did not wish to be different from others or to receive gifts that were not given to all men. He tried to drive away the experiences by going to the cinema, but found that however he might keep his attention on the screen, the inner state would return and remind him that a quite different process was present in him also. He sought, by throwing himself wholeheartedly into his pRoféssional duties and his family life, to bring about the cessation of his inner experiences. During this time he studied accountancy more seriously, and five children, two boys and three girls, were born to him and his wife, whom he had married in 1922.

The nightly visitations ceased early in 1928, and for the next five years he almost ceased to be aware of the inward

48

working that had started in his twenty-fourth year. Nevertheless during this time his friends began to resort to him for advice and help, recognizing that he had the word of truth which could penetrate to their real needs. He was not regarded at that time as being above the ordinary human stature, but as a man of exceptional insight and understanding of his fellow men and their problems. As the years passed he came himself to feel that he had found his place, and although he realized that his abilities were wasted as a book-keeper in a small municipal office, he had no ambition to achieve worldly success.

To avoid any misunderstanding as to the nature of Pak Subuh's experiences between the ages of sixteen and thirty-two, it may be said that during the three years from twenty-four to twenty-seven, the spiritual exercises, subsequently given to thousands of others, were enacted in him almost nightly and he experienced in himself the completion of the four stages of purification to be described later. Indications are often received in the exercises that show what is necessary for one's own inner and outer life. One example cited by Pak Subuh, from his own experience, may give some idea of the combination of symbolic or pictorial representation with a more direct prehension that frequently occurs. About one year after the process started in him, Muhammad Subuh began to be troubled by his inability to understand the meaning of his experiences and the impossibility of receiving help from any outside source. One night, he received the answers that he needed, and realized also that he was neither to receive nor to transmit a new 'teaching'.

This raised a new question for him. He was fully aware of the importance of the transformation that was taking place in his own nature, but he felt that it could not be right that he alone should receive the contact. If he was not to teach anything, how was his experience to be transmitted to others? He felt that he would rather not receive it at all, than enjoy it alone.

After some time, he received clear indications that he had been chosen as a means whereby everyone who wished to do so could receive exactly the same contact and pass through the

49

same process of transformation as he had himself. This is indeed what occurred later, and herein lies the crucial and extraordinary quality of Subud that distinguishes it from any other kind of spiritual work of which I have heard or read - namely, that it can be transmitted integrally and without diminution from one human being to another. This is contrary to reason, for it seems to violate the principle, exemplified in the second law of thermodynamics and the aging of living beings, that every irreversible action must involve a diminution of quality or intensity. Therefore the *contact* is what matters, since, unless it be made directly from the source, diminution, adulteration and distortion are inevitable. Such is the common lot of all teachings, and it can well be understood that Muhammad Subuh found himself shrinking from the possibility that he might become a teacher, having the contact himself and seeing others deprived of it.

When he reached his thirty-second year, Muhammad Subuh had become, to all appearance, a normal householder busied with the cares of a growing family and his everyday duties. On the night of 21st/22nd June, 1933, there occurred an event of which it seems wrong even to attempt a description. We have heard Pak Subuh speak of it several times, but always in conditions when our own consciousness was set free from its usual limitations. Nevertheless, this date is so important for the history of Subud that it is necessary to record the fact that on this day Muhammad Subuh became aware of the true significance of his life on earth. He understood that it was his mission and his task to transmit to everyone who asked for it the inner working of the spirit that he himself had received.

3. Transmission of the Contact

From this time onward, Pak Subuh began to withdraw from his official duties; and, after the time needed to train his successor, resigned from government service, and devoted himself thenceforward to the transmission of the spiritual contact. The first to receive it was the chief disciple of the

Nakshi Sheikh to whom he had gone for explanations. Later the Sheikh himself, by then a very old man, set out on a journey to receive the latihan, but died before he could meet Pak Subuh again.

Since Pak Subuh himself made no attempt to propagate a teaching, and indeed repudiated the role of teacher, the spreading of his work was at first very slow. Only a few friends and former fellow-seekers came to him, and of these not many could grasp the simplicity and universality of what he had to give. It was not until 1941, when Java was soon to be occupied by the Japanese, that news of the benefits bodily and spiritual obtained in the latihan began to spread abroad. The Japanese occupation once again retarded the extension of the movement and it was not until after the war that it moved to Jogjakarta, the capital of one of the ancient kingdoms of Java.

An incident of the Japanese occupation illustrates both Pak Subuh's submission and the difference between his role and that of a teacher. At one time, it appeared that no one's life was safe in Java, and Pak Subuh thought that it might perhaps be his duty to write down all that had been revealed to him concerning human and cosmic mysteries, lest it all be lost if he should prematurely leave the earthly scene. He accordingly set himself to write, and in six months had completed twelve note books of manuscript. Soon afterwards he left home to spend a few weeks in another town. When he returned he found that the family, being short of fuel, and mistaking his manuscript for waste paper, had burned it all. He realized that this was an indication that he was not intended to transmit a teaching and wrote no more of the mysteries of heaven and earth.

4. The Foundation of Subud

On 1st February, 1947, Subud was established in Jogjakarta as a Brotherhood with simple statutes, the main theme of which was that the aim of the movement is to enable people of all races and creeds to share in the worship of God. For this no organization is needed, but since we have to live in the world, it is necessary to provide external conditions for a harmonious social life. The wording of the preamble to the original statutes gives an idea of Pak Subuh's intention in founding it:

Preamble to the Statutes of the First Subud Brotherhood 1947.

"Inasmuch as we are certain with all our being that it is the Will of God that we should rightly fulfil our earthly obligations, we must in the conduct of worldly affairs make the fullest use of all the instruments bestowed upon us for that purpose by Divine Decree.

"Inasmuch also as, for the perfecting of eternal life, we have been endowed by God with a Spiritual Essence, this essence also requires both the means and the opportunities necessary for its harmonious development in such a manner as to give true meaning and significance to all our inner impulses and outer activities in the station that we happen to occupy in life, as well as in our relationships with our fellow men, in our attitude towards ourselves and also in our way upon the path that will lead us back towards our Source.

"In the course of our search for Spiritual Development and in our desire to share with all Mankind the common aim of true Worship of God, we are confronted with the world and with its questions. Upon the path, there thus arise sundry questions concerning, for example, the formation of groups and hence of directors and those under direction, the respective needs of young and old - in general, all questions that concern the organization of people who are brought together by a common aim: namely, in this instance, that of achieving unity of understanding leading to the performance of our duties in perfect harmony of intention and action."

5. Susila Budhi Dharma

Soon after the foundation of Subud, Pak Subuh was inspired to write a lengthy poem in high Javanese with the title 'Susila Budhi Dharma'. The subject matter of the poem is the array of forces that act upon man during his life on earth. A recurring theme is the working of the latihan as a means of liberating man from the sway of all the lower forces, and of bringing them under his control.

High Javanese is rapidly becoming a dead language, known only to those of royal or noble descent, and even among these it is now seldom taught to children. Those who know the language affirm that the poem Susila Budhi Dharma is a literary masterpiece, but we read it only in an Indonesian version which is a prose interpretation of the contents of the poem, written by Pak Subuh himself. The book is intended for the guidance of those who follow the Subud spiritual exercises. When carefully studied, it proves to contain a profound psychological analysis of the forces - conscious and sub-conscious - that dominate human life, and shows how these forces are gradually purified and harmonized when thought is put aside and the inner consciousness of man is awakened. True to the principle that one should not attempt to put into words that which is beyond the mind, Pak Subuh stops the exposition at the point where the human consciousness begins to become aware of the Divine Mysteries.

6. The Expansion of Subud

After the independence of Indonesia was proclaimed in 1949, Subud first began to acquire an international character. Husein Rofé arrived in Java early in 1950 and soon was received as a member of Subud. After spending nearly two years as a member of Pak Subuh's own household, Rofé became an active missionary and helped to make Subud known, first in Indonesian islands outside Java and later in the Far Eastern countries. According to letters received from people in Singapore and Hong Kong who met Rofé at that time, it seems that his journeys were made under conditions of extreme personal hardship and at first showed very little fruit. It was at this time that news of Subud first began to reach Western countries, chiefly through articles written by Rofé for various Islamic journals. Several Dutch and other European people came to the latihan. By 1954, branches had been established in several of the Indonesian islands, in Hong Kong, and in Japan. An article by Rofé attracted the attention of Meredith Starr, a well-known authority on methods of spiritual training, then living in Cyprus. Starr invited Rofé to Cyprus. Arriving there towards the end of 1955, he transmitted the latihan to a number of interested people. This in turn led to the decision that Rofé should come to England, where he arrived in the summer of 1956.

Meanwhile, the expansion of Subud in the Indonesian Islands was proceeding steadily. More than two thousand men and women had received the latihan, which was regularly practised in Djakarta, the capital, as well as in many outlying places. Reports of remarkable cures of illnesses were undoubtedly one of the main factors in the growing interest in Subud. On the whole, the orthodox Moslem authorities, the Ulema, were lukewarm towards a movement so catholic in its scope as Subud. Pak Subuh did not make, and has never made, any distinctions of race or creed among those accepted for the latihan, emphasizing that Subud is not a new religion nor a system of thought, but simply a means whereby the spiritual life can be awakened and strengthened in each person according to his or her personal faith and practice. Since it is very hard for most people to separate the pure religious experience as such from some particular dogma concerning Divine Mysteries, the simple message of Subud often seems like a call to abandon, or at least to change one's own beliefs and practices. It is only by degrees that the real significance of Subud as the way to find the true content of every teaching and every creed becomes apparent. This may perhaps account for its relatively slow progress in the twenty-one years from 1933 to 1954.

7. Subud in England

When Subud came to England, it found a propitious soil among many hundreds of followers of Gurdjieff's system for the Harmonious Developments of Man. Gurdjieff's system is catholic, and founded on the belief that in all men there is the potentiality of a conscious awakening of the powers that can remain dormant throughout life. Thus, Gurdjieff's pupils were familiar with the notion that man is unaware of his true nature, which can be developed and perfected only by a lengthy conscious process.

No previous preparation or spiritual training is required for admission to the Subud latihan, and its action is as effectual in those who have had little or no experience of spiritual exercises as in those who have devoted all their lives to such matters. Nevertheless, it also cannot be gainsaid that the working of Subud is mysterious and incomprehensible to the logical thought of the average cultured man or woman of our times. For those who have already grasped the distinction so clearly made by Gurdjieff between the higher and the lower centres, between the essence and the personality, between conscience and morality, the working of Subud, though still mysterious, is nevertheless wholly acceptable. Gurdjieff's insistence on the uselessness in the spiritual life of that which he calls the 'formatory apparatus', that is, the mechanism of associative thought and linguistic analysis, fully accords with Pak Subuh's reiterated advice to put aside efforts of thought and feeling and await the experience of a purified and therefore empty consciousness.

It was, therefore, not surprising that when Husein Rofé arrived in England he found the readiest response in a small number of men and women who for many years had studied Gurdjieff's method, but were convinced that it was not complete unless a way could be found to achieve the awakening of the higher centres of consciousness through direct contact with a Higher Source.

8. The Arrival of Pak Subuh

Muhammad Subuh with his wife and helpers arrived from Indonesia on 22nd May, 1957, and within a week had accepted an invitation from our Institute to make his headquarters while in England at Coombe Springs. Many members of the Institute were soon admitted to the latihan, and it seemed possible that all the groups in England interested in Gurdjieff's ideas would join forces in Subud. I have already described the events that led to the suspension of this expectation.

I may be forgiven if I describe one strange incident that occurred during the first week of Pak Subuh's stay at Coombe Springs. Though the house is not old, the grounds contain very ancient springs, the waters of which were believed to have healing power. In 1514, when Cardinal Wolsey built Hampton Court Palace, he sent for an Italian engineer -reputed to be a pupil of Leonardo da Vinci - to bring water from Coombe Springs to the Palace. Numerous oak conduits lined with lead collected the waters from Coombe Hill and brought them to a central point now in our grounds where two conduit houses were erected, joined by a long subterranean tunnel. Two lead tanks were sunk in the ground to enable, so it is said, the local people to maintain the practice of dipping sick children in the water. Round the conduit houses oak trees were planted, some of which - now nearly four hundred and fifty years old - are still standing. There has always been an atmosphere of mystery and constraint about this corner of the grounds, and some have believed, that ghosts or troubled spirits haunted it. I myself, going to the springs in the middle of the night, have often experienced a strange unease, as if entities both friendly and unfriendly were aware of my presence.

In the middle of June, a sense of oppression and foreboding seemed to have invaded Coombe Springs. One evening, there was an extraordinary force present in the latihan. Everyone living at Coombe went to bed with the feeling that they had been witness of some gigantic though invisible struggle. At about three o'clock in the morning, nearly all the fifty or so people living at Coombe Springs were awakened by the sound of an explosion that was like a thunderclap in the very grounds, and yet somehow different. Someone compared it the next day to the sound she had heard during the war of an aircraft exploding overhead. It transpired that neighbours in the adjoining houses had heard nothing. And yet one woman living ten miles away telephoned the next morning to say that she had heard the explosion at three o'clock and had somehow connected it with Coombe Springs. Everyone noticed next day that the atmosphere had lightened and that the sense of oppression had entirely disappeared.

When Pak Subuh was asked about this, he explained that evil forces had been resisting the coming of Subud to Coombe, but that they had now been destroyed. Such incidents can mean little to those who hear of them at second hand. They are not 'evidence' of anything; but those who were present that evening could not doubt that some kind of battle had been waged and that the 'good' forces had conquered. This is but one of the many strange experiences that occurred both to individuals and to groups of people during the months of June and July. I have included it only so that the record may be reasonably complete.

These were weeks of intense activity that made us recognize the change of tempo that is characteristic of Subud. One of Ouspensky's former pupils having, in April 1957, attended a film of some of the Gurdjieff rhythmic dances at which nearly a thousand of his followers were present, remarked that it had taken thirty-six years since Ouspensky first came to England in 1921 for the movement to grow from forty to a thousand members, and predicted that to establish Subud in the West might take no less time. In the event, Subud has established itself in England in fewer weeks than other movements have taken years. It is already known throughout the world, and the chief difficulty is to keep pace with its growth.

9. The 'Healing' of Eva Bartok

Obvious contributory factors to the growth of Subud have been, first, that several hundred people were able, at least a little, to understand the significance of Subud, and second, the publicity given by the press in November 1957 to the circumstances attending the birth of Eva Bartok's child Deana. A far more important reason for the spreading of Subud has been the rapid and unmistakable action of the latihan upon all sorts and conditions of men and women. The greater number of those who have come to the latihan after the initial stages have done

57

so on account of the clearly visible changes for the better in their friends and relatives who had already started.

In view of the interest that has been aroused in the case of Eva Bartok and the misleading accounts that have appeared in the press, it may be wise to include here the history of the events as we witnessed them ourselves. Miss Bartok has for several years been interested in Gurdjieff's method, and had impressed us by the tenacity with which she has held to the work under the most adverse life circumstances. A refugee from Hungary at the time of the Communist occupation in 1946, exposed inevitably to pressures that would either have turned the head or ruined the character of most women, she retained nevertheless her religious faith and the belief that a way of inner life could be found. The more sensational events of her life are well known and need not be recounted. Her first chance of making a film in Hollywood, still the Mecca of film stars, came in the summer of 1956, but she went there a tired and distressed young woman, having failed to achieve a harmonious marriage with a charming and brilliant, but headstrong, German film actor. In April 1957 she telephoned to me from Hollywood to say that she was very ill, and that a serious operation was unavoidable.

She wished to have the operation in England, but only after she had spoken to me about preparing for death. As she was speaking, a clear indication came to me that she was destined to be cured through Subud, and that this would have many consequences that I foresaw with very mixed feelings. Ever since April 1946, when the Institute was founded at Coombe Springs, we have carefully avoided publicity, and indeed had been remarkably successful in turning aside requests for permission to photograph and write articles upon our work. It had always appeared to us that spiritual work could prosper only if it were kept out of the limelight. At that time I did not understand that Subud was under different laws from those of most spiritual undertakings.

Miss Bartok reached England on 19th May, a week before Pak Subuh arrived, and having grown considerably worse consulted two surgeons, both of whom appear to have advised her very earnestly to submit to an operation without delay. Although her disease was not malignant, there was a danger of complications that might prove fatal.

In this situation a very grave decision had to be taken: one that I would not wish to be faced with again. A young woman was threatened on the one hand with the danger of fatal complications, and on the other with the virtual certainty that if she had the operation she would lose her child and even all hopes of motherhood. There was the possibility that the Subud latihan might save her. Pak Subuh himself had not then left Java, and our only direct evidence of the healing power of Subud came from three or four cases in the original small group, whose members had found an undoubted improvement in their health. The position was explained to Miss Bartok, and she elected to wait, saying that it seemed that she had now the possibility of the spiritual awakening for which she had been waiting since her early youth, and that she would take any risk rather than lose this chance.

When I was driving Pak Subuh to London from the airport I told him of Eva Bartok's situation. After waiting, as he always does when confronting serious questions, for an inner indication, Pak Subuh said that she should receive the latihan, and for this she should be moved down to Coombe Springs. The next day Pak Subuh sent his wife Ibu and Ismana Achmad to the Lodge at Coombe Springs where Miss Bartok was staying with Mrs. Elizabeth Howard. She was thus the first person in Europe to receive the latihan directly from Ibu Subuh. The only visible change was a relief of certain distressing symptoms, and for a fortnight very little seemed to be happening. Her own doctor, who saw her daily, confirmed that she was in no immediate danger, but added his own advice to the recommendations of her surgeon that she should agree to the operation as soon as possible. She accepted this advice, and arrangements were made for her to enter a London hospital on the evening of 10th June.

During these nineteen days Pak Subuh himself did not once see Miss Bartok. The absence of any apparent improvement in the clinical symptoms only seemed to emphasize the reality of the inner psychic change. Everyone who saw Miss Bartok at this time was impressed by the change in her expression, and by the serenity with which she was facing the prospect of a dangerous operation. It is here worth remarking that several months later a distinguished prelate who asked for information about Subud affirmed that his interest had been aroused by the unmistakable spiritual transformation that was revealed by the photographs he had seen of Miss Bartok before and after she came to Subud.

When the hospital arrangements were reported to Pak Subuh on the morning of 10th June, he personally went down to the Lodge, and with Ibu, Ismana, Elizabeth Howard and myself, entered into the latihan standing round Miss Bartok's bed. This was for the two English people the first demonstration of the indescribable power of the Subud latihan. The little bedroom was charged with energy that annihilated all personal feeling and produced a state of consciousness in which all seemed to be sharing in one and the same experience as the sick woman.

We felt the same physical pains, the same fears and the same weak but growing faith in the power of God. None of us could have said how long the experience lasted, but afterwards we found that it was barely forty minutes. Then without having spoken a word Pak Subuh went away. Miss Bartok herself was in acute pain which persisted through the day. When Pak Subuh was consulted, he said, "Let her doctor give her a good sedative. It will not interfere with the exercise. Now the crisis is over, and she will not need an operation."

It occurred as he predicted. From the morning of 11th June, Miss Bartok's condition began to improve, and within three weeks she was confident that she would have a living child. This was soon to be confirmed by experienced obstetric surgeons, and the baby was successfully delivered in October and is strong and thriving.

For those of us who were witnesses of the whole event, it was far more astonishing than can be described in words. It was not the fact of a cure that impressed us, but the unmistakable evidence that the psychic or spiritual change preceded the somatic. The healing of a distressed soul is more remarkable than recovering from an illness. When one sees the two in juxtaposition and can follow the course of the transition from the psychic to the somatic, one cannot doubt that a very great and a very good force is at work. Since then we have seen many other such cases, and the link between the psychic and the somatic has always been clearly in evidence.

10. Subud in Europe

The principle that the Subud contact can be given only in response to a request extends also to its entry into new places. When he came to England, Pak Subuh had expressed his intention of returning home within three months unless invited to some other country. We did not at first understand the significance of this declaration, as we supposed that, like most people, he would make his own plans and go where he thought best. In July a few members of our Dutch group came to Coombe Springs to be opened and invited him to go to Holland, where many who could not travel to England wished to receive the contact.

He then explained that he had received no indication from within that he should go to Holland but, in the absence of an invitation to Germany or to America, both of which he expected, he would go to Holland. We thus began to learn something of the extent to which Pak Subuh is obedient to the command to undertake nothing of his own volition.

On the 1st September the Indonesian party went to Holland for a visit of six weeks, and new branches of Subud were established at the Hague and in Eindhoven. These have grown out of groups studying Gurdjieff's system and connected for many years with Coombe Springs. During this time I went to Germany, having spoken of Subud to friends in Stuttgart,

Munich and Nuremberg, and returned with a letter of invitation signed by Frau Ruth Grüson, Count Manfred Keyserling and Baron Christopher von Tucher. On 16th December, Pak Subuh went to Munich where he remained for seven weeks, apart from a short visit to Zurich, St. Gallen and Berne in Switzerland. During this time the German press published sensational but not unfriendly stories of Subud. The effect of the publicity was to deter many serious people from coming; nevertheless more than two hundred were opened in Munich and more than a hundred in Switzerland. Active Subud centres were established in Munich, Zurich and St. Gallen.

The heaviest burden both during and after the visit fell on Ruth Grüson, herself a follower of the work at Coombe Springs of many years' standing. To those who knew how seriously ill she had been previously it was impressive to witness the new strength with which Frau Grüson was endowed. We saw also how, lacking any pre-existing organization, Subud in Germany began to take an external form that corresponded to the needs of the German character.

Invitations were now being received from all over Europe: from France, Norway, Italy, Spain and Greece. But Pak Subuh was waiting for something to come from America. Some of us had written to friends in the United States, but without a personal visit it seemed impossible to convey the significance of Subud, and we began to prepare for Pak Subuh's return by way of Cyprus and Turkey, leaving the New World to a later visit.

11. The Influx from Overseas

The story of the coming of Subud would not be complete without reference to the remarkable influx of people from all parts of the world - in many cases without prior knowledge of what they were to find. A mere list of the countries from which men and women have set out to find Pak Subuh is sufficiently impressive. They include Singapore, India, Ceylon, Pakistan, Turkey, Cyprus, Italy, Switzerland, France, Spain, Holland, Germany, Sweden and Norway, Morocco, Egypt, Nigeria,

Kenya, Ghana, South Africa, Canada and the United States, and finally two came from Kodiak Island in the North Pacific, having travelled 11,300 miles. But the circumstances of the visits were more extraordinary than their number and variety. One or two examples must suffice.

An Indian lady, Mrs. Bulbul Arnold, came to Coombe Springs at the suggestion of her sister-in-law, and asked for advice on behalf of her husband, who was suffering from an acute asthma with complications for which no medical remedy had been found. He had been flown to Switzerland to see a famous specialist, but could get only temporary relief. In the outcome both husband and wife joined Pak Subuh in Holland, and not only was Mr. Arnold's condition radically improved, but remarkable changes occurred in their lives that have already benefited many others.

About the same time, a well-known journalist from Ceylon felt during June a strong urge to come to England, although he had no clear business reasons for leaving Ceylon. On arrival, he telephoned to Coombe Springs, and that evening was told about Subud and at once recognized that it was for this that he had come to England. Returning home after four weeks, he was instrumental in preparing several score of people, and a letter was received inviting Pak Subuh to visit the country on his way back to Indonesia. In January 1958, Subud was taken to Ceylon by lcksan Ahmad and Bulbul Arnold, and within three weeks three hundred and twenty-six people had been admitted to the latihan. Thus from two apparently unconnected and personal impulses, Subud has reached a country where the sense of expectancy in recent years has been exceptionally strong.

George Cornelius, who had come in 1940 to Gurdjieff's work while working in the office of the American Naval Attaché in London, had retired with his wife Mary to Kodiak Island, and we had little news of them for seven years. There seemed to be no likelihood of their returning to England. Friends at Coombe Springs had written to Mary about Subud, but her impressions had apparently been unfavourable. Nevertheless, in November

1957, both George and Mary had begun to feel unaccountably drawn towards England. News of her mother's illness was a reason for Mary to make the journey, but her husband was occupied with a new business undertaking and could not get away. Suddenly an unexpected opportunity presented itself - heralded, as has often happened, by a symbolic dream. When they arrived in England, Mary Cornelius said that she did not wish to come near Coombe Springs for fear of becoming involved. Almost in spite of themselves, both did come, and were so strongly impressed by the change that they found in their friends whom they had known seven years before, that they asked to be opened. In both there was an unusually quick and positive response, and they returned to Kodiak after a few weeks convinced that their coming to England had been providentially ordered. I have recounted this story to illustrate what frequently occurs - the personality is reluctant and wishes to escape, but the essence is drawn by a force that cannot be denied.

Such events taken singly could scarcely be evidence of a conscious directing power working behind the scenes in Subud. When scores of similar cases can be cited, it is still possible to invoke coincidence or the natural tendency of man to generalize from inadequate premises. When taken in conjunction with the altogether unusual and inexplicable experience of more than a thousand people from many races and religions drawn from all parts of the world, it is hard to explain the events except by invoking the action of a Conscious Angelic Power, the presence of which man himself in his ordinary states of awareness and sensitivity does not even suspect.

It should not be inferred that all who come to Subud continue with the latihan. A proportion - less than one tenth - go away almost at once, either because they are afraid or because they expect some strange or miraculous experience which they do not find. The chief obstacle is the tendency to 'compare' and so to be influenced by what appears to be happening to other people. Indeed with so many reasons for giving up, it is really remarkable that so high a proportion has remained.

Subud has made its mark in Europe more rapidly and more surely than any other movement that, having originated in some remote Asiatic country, has been brought to the West. Once, when an Englishman commented to Pak Subuh upon this rapid assimilation of a foreign movement, he replied: "Subud is not foreign. It belongs to no country, just as it belongs to no race or creed. It did not 'originate' in the East, and it did not 'come' to the West. It comes from the Spirit of God, which is nowhere a stranger. So when we arrived in England we did not feel ourselves as foreigners, nor did you feel that we were strangers from a strange land. From the beginning we could be like brothers, because there is one and only One Spirit that works in us all. That is the true meaning of Subud."

12. Subud goes round the World

Before the end of January 1958, an invitation to San Francisco was received from John Cooke, a descendent of the Cooke who was one of the first missionaries to Hawaii, whose life is a hardly credible story of adventure of the spirit. Pak Subuh promptly accepted and decided to pass over the eastern states and bring Subud straight to California. A Canadian, Bob Prestie, went ahead and I followed a week later with Elizabeth Howard. Pak Subuh and his party arrived in San Francisco on 22nd March, just ten months after his first landing in England.

Within a few weeks, centres had been started in San Francisco, Los Angeles, Carmel and in Sacramento, the State capital. In California, Subud has had to overcome a new kind of obstacle, due to the disillusionment of thousands who had sought for a spiritual way of life and had over-enthusiastically embraced the innumerable new movements and sects promising quick and easy ways of achieving salvation or enlightenment that had come to the west coast of America during the past thirty years. It was very natural that Subud should appear as just another such movement, and that Californians should be wary and suspicious in their approach to it.

65

With his usual insight into local conditions before even encountering them, Pak Subuh had recommended that in the U.S.A. all publicity should be avoided; and it is remarkable that throughout our two months' stay only one mention of Subud should appear in the American press. Nevertheless, men and women from all sections of the community began to arrive and between three and four hundred people received the contact. The openness and sincerity of Americans make them responsive to Subud, and before we left it was clear that a strong nucleus of helpers had been formed in three centres. Moreover, people were beginning to hear of Subud in other States and Pak Subuh was invited to go to the midwest and east and south, and even to Canada.

However, he had a fixed date to keep in Java on 10th June and we expected him to go straight back. Then an invitation was quite unexpectedly received from Australia, from Dr. Philip Groves, leader of a group that for years had been working according to Gurdjieff's system and methods. The letter conveyed a note of urgent pleading for help that could not be dismissed, and Pak Subuh announced that he would spend a week in Sydney. Realizing that the time would be too short to establish a viable centre, I offered to go before him, although this meant deferring important tasks awaiting me in England.

Mrs. Howard, with her two sons, and I accordingly left for Sydney on 3rd May and, after two days in Honolulu where we met some of John Cooke's family, who asked to hear about Subud, we reached Sydney on 7th May. There we found an extraordinary situation; the Australian press were making a sensation of Subud and we had to face a posse of reporters, T.V. cameras and radio interviewers before we could meet some fifty men and women waiting to be opened the very first night of our arrival.

So began the most strenuous month since the previous June. Pak Subuh came on 28th May and we all left on 7th June. During the month more than five hundred were opened. Most of the time we were subjected to a flood of publicity, some offensive, some facetious and some serious. The Australians who came to Subud were amazing in their sincerity and fortitude under really difficult conditions. Indeed, it was evident that the Power behind Subud would work with greater intensity the greater the outward difficulties. People came from all over the continent - a small group flew 3,000 miles from Perth to receive the contact. Pak Subuh himself gave more than in any other city, receiving numerous visitors every morning, bringing them rapidly forward to a deeper understanding of the latihan. Several men and women of outstanding spiritual qualities came to Subud and now form a nucleus of centres in Australia that will be important in the future.

From Sydney we travelled - as it happened, in the same plane with Sri Meher Baba, the Indian Spiritual Leader - to Djakarta where we stayed eight days, visiting Jogjakarta, where Susila Budhi Dharma was written, and Semarang, near the birthplace of Pak Subuh. We were received in the same house by the river, where in 1933 Pak Subuh received his greatest experiences and the place where the contact was first given to the pupils of Sheikh Abdurrahman. In each of the centres we visited, we could verify the deep and lasting action of Subud on all levels of the human organism and psyche in those who had been following the latihan for many years. To say that there was nothing foreign in living and exercising with Javanese and Sumatrans only half-describes the conviction that was steadily growing in us that Subud is a truly human action that goes far deeper than any differences of race or creed or even of personal character and qualities.

This conviction was reinforced in Singapore, where most of the Subud members are Chinese and Indian. Never before having known intimately any Chinese, I was impressed by what I can only describe as the 'inner strength' of the Chinese. They come to Subud more directly than we do, but they need it no less. Though it is hazardous to generalize from fifty individuals about a nation of five hundred millions, I formed the impression that the Chinese will more readily accept a religious experience that can be shared by all races and creeds than many other races of mankind. If I am right in my feeling that the Chinese people in general - and not just a few individuals - have an exceptional strength in respect of human qualities, then China must have a supremely important part to play in the spiritual regeneration of mankind.

We arrived in Ceylon to find a nation still deeply shocked by the recent communal riots. We saw many Tamil shops and even whole areas in remote villages burnt to the ground and heard pitiful stories of beatings and murders - all done, as one devout Buddhist said sadly, "in the name of the Compassionate One".

The external conditions only served to throw into relief the absence of any sense of conflict between the Buddhist, Tamil, Muslim and Christian members who share in the Subud exercises. One story of the 'protection' that covers those who surrender their personal will in the latihan is typical of many. A Tamil civil servant was going to work by tram on the worst day of the riots. The tram was stopped by a crowd of Cinghalese who started to drag out and beat up the Tamil occupants. The Subud member found that the exercise started in him spontaneously, and continued to sit quietly. Although his Tamil features are particularly evident, he was not noticed by the rioters who dragged all the other Tamils out of the tram while he was left in peace. He gained such confidence from this experience that he refused to go into hiding, and he never was molested. Indeed, not one Tamil belonging to Subud was touched throughout the troubles.

The stay in Ceylon was crowded with strong experiences which brought home to us both the strength of the 'sub-human' forces that are in us all against our own will, and also the purifying and strengthening action of the latihan.

Short visits to India, Pakistan, Switzerland and Germany completed an experience that brought us in touch with half the races of the world. My impressions of India are based on too few contacts and too short a time to be worth recording, but

Pak Subuh himself has referred to the special role of India and the presence there of men of exceptional spiritual qualities who are aware of the coming of Subud.

The social and political tensions that oppress all mankind become more and more acute. The reconciling power of Subud has shown itself on a very small scale - having touched a few thousand people spread through a dozen countries. It has come into the world, but no one can yet tell what it may do in the future to allay the fears and renew the hopes of mankind.

4. WORKING FROM WITHOUT AND FROM WITHIN

1. Two Principles of Existence

THE significance of Subud can be understood only if we recognize the distinction between two processes by which man can fulfil his destiny here on earth. The first can be called 'working from without' and it comprises all the actions undertaken by a man directed towards an ideal formed in him as a result of external influences. Such actions can range from conforming to a code of behaviour dictated by religious convictions or by social responsibility, to the search for a complete inner transformation or liberation by way of some self-imposed spiritual discipline of effort and suffering. The second process can be called 'working from within', and it operates from some source within man himself. In its true sense, working from within is the action of Divine Grace operating in the depths of the human soul. There can, however, be other modes of spontaneous inner working where the contact with the Source is indirect only.

This distinction is an ancient one, for it is the origin of all theological controversies concerning salvation by works and salvation by faith. The distinction is beyond human understanding, for it involves comparison between two completely unlike factors or effects. We can see and know what it means to go by the way of effort and suffering. Even when efforts are directed towards a right state of consciousness, they are not different in their essential character from the muscular efforts made by a ploughman or a blacksmith. All effort requires attention, choice, decision and persistence and these are operations of the will of man. It is quite impossible to reduce the action of Grace to similar terms, for it does not operate from but by the free consent of the will of man.

For those who are familiar with the distinction between

time and eternity, it is possible to say that all working from without is temporal, but that the action of Grace is eternal and can never be observed as an event.[1] Man in his ordinary state of consciousness is 'eternity-blind' and is unaware that there are different levels in eternity. Unconsciously he projects all his experience on to the level of sensation and thought, and this creates a tendency to believe in 'works' which can be seen, and to misunderstand the very nature of 'faith'.

2. The Human Personality

Before birth, all influences that act upon the foetus are of human or superhuman origin - apart from the possibility that animal soul-substance may enter at conception. After birth, the first influences are animal in character. They are mainly concerned with warmth and food and come from the mother or some other large mammal such as a cow. After a few weeks the child begins to be aware of its own body, first however with the animal and vegetative functions, and only much later does it begin to recognize material objects and to acquire a relationship with the inanimate world. It can be said that the incarnation of the human spirit is not complete until it recognizes the material world as the environment in which its life-pattern on earth is to be worked out.

The world of our familiar experience is a world of material objects - including of course living animal and human bodies - but this is not the world entered by the new-born child. That world is not visible and tangible - for the child does not yet know what seeing and touching are. It is a series of worlds composed of human, animal and vegetable essences, in which forces are working that cannot be reduced to the play of atoms and quanta.

We are not yet ready to discuss these unseen worlds, and must pass to the arising of the common experience of man as a person. The new-born child is impersonal, but very soon people about it begin to elicit personal reactions. From them it learns

---

1   cf. *The Dramatic Universe*, Vol. I, p. 161.

that its cries can attract attention. They engage its interest in them as persons. Thus, little by little, a new personality is formed. This is an artificial construction that is produced by influences completely different from those that formed the essence. The personality comprises all that one learns from the outside world; and, since the child learns mainly from or with the help of other people, the personality inevitably bears the imprint of all the other personalities that it meets during its formative years.

The main instruments of the personality are the associative mechanism of the cerebral hemispheres, that is what we usually call the 'brain', together with the complex apparatus for emotional and instinctive reactions furnished by the autonomic nervous system and the endocrine glands. The head brain is supplied with means for storing sense impressions, and for sorting and classifying them with the help of signs. Signs take the form of language, which again the child learns from other people. Although sense impressions themselves are received directly, they are put into the form of usable memories almost entirely by what is learned from others. Thus the innate capacity of the essence to perceive the real world is gradually supplanted and replaced by thinking about sense impressions with the help of language.

3. The Variety of Influences that act on Man

A simple but valuable distinction can be made between two kinds of external influences that act upon man. This is based on the assumption that there are levels of experience that have a direct contact with real or essential worlds higher than this earth. These influences are transmitted through human sources, and their effect is to awaken in man the realization that his destiny is not to live, grow old and die and perish on this earth, but to attain the conscious freedom or immortality of the human soul as the vehicle of the spirit.

Some such assumption is common to· all religions and to all philosophies that acknowledge God as the Creator and

Ruler of all worlds. But, as Kant showed in his Critique of Practical Reason, it is even prior to belief in God, for it derives from the conviction that we men have an obligation to live our lives according to certain standards that are in themselves of more than human origin. This obligation, the categorical imperative, is not reached by way of thought or even experience, but, because it comes from within ourselves, it is the only sound foundation for all ethics and all morality. If it is denied, then ethics reduces to the unworkable doctrine of the 'greatest good of the greatest number', that would find few defenders or advocates today.

We can all see that we live under two kinds of influence which differ, not merely in their form, but in their origin, their action and their result. They can be described as the worldly and the other-worldly, as the temporal and the eternal, as the material and the spiritual, and as the religious and the irreligious. But we must make sure that such names do not mislead us. It is by their origin, their action and their results that such influences must be judged. The first kind originate in the mind and feelings of men who see only the visible world. They act upon the personality to strengthen its belief that there is no other world but this. The result of their action is to bind man to the earth and deprive him of his essential birthright. The influences of the second kind originate beyond the mind and feelings of man, and they act to undermine and eventually to destroy the slavery of the personality. Their result is to open man's eyes to the possibility, latent in his essence, of dying to this world and of rebirth to another and better world.

Since influences of the first kind leave the psychic nature of man unchanged, they have been called *psycho-static*. The second kind set the psyche in motion upon a path that can lead to an endless progress, and so have been called *psycho-kinetic*.[1] Unless this distinction is clearly understood and remembered, we are likely to fall into the common error of supposing that we can reach paradise or enter the Kingdom of Heaven -

---

[1]   cf, *The Crisis in Human Affairs*, pp. 131-44. p

remaining such as we are. All the parables of Jesus concerning the Kingdom of Heaven agree as to the need to pay a great price for it. It is still more strongly expressed in the phrase "except ye be born again, ye shall in no wise enter the Kingdom". The words *in no wise* - in Greek οὐδέποτε - emphasize with all the authority of the Son of Man that there is no possible way of attaining the eternal world and the everlasting life of the soul except by death and resurrection here in this present life. The same warning was given by God through Moses in the words of Deuteronomy, "Behold I have set before you this day life and death, blessing and cursing - choose therefore life that thou and thy seed may live." The Word of God revealed to Muhammad gives the same warning, "Submit to no power but God, lest thou be of those consigned to torment" (Sura 26).

4. The Twofold Flow of Influences

All the scriptures insist upon the need for a positive, conscious and decisive act of choice, and it is the disregard of this uncompromising demand that has in all ages caused the downfall of religion.

We thus come to the question of how the choice is made. The personality is formed under influences of both kinds, and it has no power of distinguishing between them. But the essence has elements that do not belong to the temporal, visible world. By the action of those elements each man has an urge to seek for the invisible, the imperishable and the eternal. In so far, therefore, as the essence is not wholly trapped in the personality, there arises a discrimination that can recognize the value of those influences that draw man towards the fulfilment of his essential destiny.

We are drawn towards eternal life because there is in each of us a part of our being that is eternal. But that part is potential only, and it is covered and closed by the experiences, memories, desires and thoughts of the personality. So long as we live in our personality the essential reality sleeps. If the awakening comes in the personality there remains a long process of preparation and purification before the way to the essence is opened. If the awakening comes in the essence the same process is still necessary, but it is accomplished through the far greater powers that operate in the essence. These are not so much two *ways* as two opposing *directions of flow of forces*. The origin of the force is always the same - it is the Will of God that man should be enabled to return to his Source - but when the force flows in from the outside, it has first to pass through many channels, each of which takes something from it and adds something to it, so that by the time it reaches the human individual it is not and cannot be pure. When the force flows from within, it enters the spirit of man directly in its full and perfect purity - so awakening the soul to consciousness of the Presence and the Power of God. Herein lies the difference between justification by works and justification by faith. The first is contingent and hazardous, the second is complete and infallible.

5. Working from Without

We are not concerned with theories or explanations, but with the actual experience of the man or woman who chooses to fulfil his or her true destiny. The choice is made not once but incessantly, until complete unity of being is attained, and he is able to choose finally and utterly with the whole of himself. It is very necessary that we should realize that the final choice is indeed final, and that it belongs to the end and not to the beginning of the way. Even in those ascetic orders which require complete renunciation of the world and all external attachments, and which, because of the austerity of their rules, impose a long period of probation upon their aspirants, it is well understood that the habit does not make the monk and that choice, which is really the same as repentance, must continue to the very end.

When we represent to ourselves an ideal state of being that is remote from what we now are and yet inherently attainable, we may choose to impose on ourselves a discipline that will bring us nearer to the ideal. This is the type of all 'working from without'. Even the *Imitatio Christi* is working from without, for Christ as the ideal Man is a representation of our own minds, and the efforts we make to follow in His footsteps are our own efforts. When the Yogi sets out to find the Great Self, the Atman that he represents to himself as identical with Brahman, the One that is beyond all form, he is still making a mental image, and his self-discipline is self-imposed.

We men and women, who fancy that we decide and act from our own choice, do not pause to ask ourselves how the possibility of choosing comes to us. If we were to do so, we should see that it has come through our senses; through what we have seen and heard and known of. If we are Christians, we are so because we have been brought up in a Christian community. If we have ideas of right and wrong, it is because from earliest childhood such ideas have reached us through hearing what people say, through watching what they do, and later through reading books and through participating in the life of the community to which we belong. As a result of all the external influences we may have formed some picture of the ideal man or woman, and we may try to make our own lives conform to that ideal. Whether the ideal is supremely great, as when we survey the life of Jesus Christ or of the Prophet Muhammad, or whether it is the glamour of a film star that attracts us, the *action* is the same. The ideal is outside of us, but somehow like us and attainable. The same applies to all ethical and moral codes. The Ten Commandments, the precepts of Confucius, the Oath of Hippocrates, the American Constitution - all are the same in principle: they prescribe forms of external behaviour that we accept willingly or unwillingly as obligatory upon ourselves, and we try more or less faithfully to discipline our lives accordingly. Receiving from without applies also to our beliefs. Each religion has its own creed, and each sect within each religion its own variant of the creed. Some are more and some are less tolerant of the beliefs of others - some are more sincere and wholehearted than others in their acceptance of the creed and dogmas of their own faith. But whatever these may be, all are received from outside in the form of verbal formulae, symbols or pictures. Nowhere is it recorded that anyone has professed the Christian or any other faith except he were first taught the creed and its meaning.

It follows, beyond possibility of dispute, that all discipline that derives from

(a) The contemplation of an ideal Man or state of existence,

(b) Obedience to commandments or moral codes, and

(c) The acceptance of creeds or dogmas of whatever form or content,

can belong only to the category of working from without.

The phrase 'working from without' must not be understood in a disparaging sense. The whole structure of human society depends upon discipline, and it is only redeemed from tyranny when there is at least as much self-imposed discipline as external constraint. But we must not overlook the limitations of any way of self-perfecting that depends upon external influences. Since it comes from our own will it can only liberate us from our own will by way of failure. Thus Kierkegaard: "To tear the will away from all finite aims and conditions requires a painful effort and this effort ceaseless repetition. And if, in addition to this, the soul has, in spite of all its striving, to be as though it simply were not, it becomes clear that the religious life signifies a dedication to suffering and to self-destruction." Thus also Gurdjieff: "We men, owing to the data crystallized in our common presences for engendering in us the Divine Impulse of Conscience, 'the-whole-of-us' and the whole of our essence, are, and must be, already in our foundation, only suffering." Gurdjieff goes on to explain that suffering is inevitable so long as we remain under the action of two incompatible sets of forces - those of the temporal world acting on our bodies and those of the eternal world that act upon our Conscience.

Those who follow any way of self-perfecting that is a form of working from without, must come to a point where they are powerless to go further because they can never, by their own will, overcome their own will. If at that point they are resolute and choose the impossible ideal in place of any possible compromise, they can die to their temporal earthly self and be born again to their eternal other-worldly self. Without such 'death and resurrection' no transformation of human nature can be completed.

There are many ways by which a man can arrive at the 'point of no return'. One of the attractions for modern people of Zen Buddhism is that it makes this position perfectly clear without dogma and without even the demand for religious faith. The works of my honoured friend Daisetz Teitaro Suzuki abound in examples of the working of such methods as the Koan exercise. The system of exercises used by St. Ignatius Loyola and his followers is equally clear in its purpose: to confront the impure sinful human soul with the image of the absolutely pure and sinless Saviour in such a manner as ultimately to destroy all hope of attaining such purity by one's own will. By such means the experience of death and resurrection is repeated at each retreat and especially during the second novitiate. The exercises taught by Gurdjieff have a more flexible quality than those used in Zen Monasteries or in the Society of Jesus. They aim at the awakening of the essence in such a manner that the ability to 'see one's own nothingness' is attained together with the strength to bear the experience. Moreover, Gurdjieff attached special importance to the balanced development of body, feelings, mind and consciousness, so that his exercises are constantly varied and adjusted to meet the changing needs of the pupil who works seriously and makes real progress.

6. Schools and Teachers

At this point I should refer to the role of 'schools' and 'teachers' in the work of self-perfecting. Any 'teaching' whether it is of the most general kind like the 'Ten Commandments', or whether it is a specialized system of self-discipline, is inevitably standardized, that is to say, it is received in a set form that is the same for all those who wish to follow it. But human beings are not *standardized*. There are very great differences in the capacities and limitations that each individual brings to the task of self-perfecting. Thus anyone who follows a fixed system of teaching must submit himself to a Procrustean bed on which he will be stretched or chopped until he is made to fit.

The world is full of psychic misfits who have attempted to adapt themselves to some standard code of discipline, whether moral or practical. Those who try to achieve the highest perfection suffer most from this deep incompatibility of their individual powers and limitations with the requirements of the way they have set themselves to follow. One of the chief causes of the decay of religion lies precisely in the general rigidity of religious discipline. Even those who are capable and desirous of adopting a severely ascetic way of life seldom find what they need in any standardized discipline.

The true significance of *schools* lies not in the possession of special methods, exercises and the like, but in having the knowledge and experience requisite to ensure that the methods are adapted to the needs of the individual. It is this understanding that marks the true spiritual director or teacher. Such teachers have always been rare, and they can hope to give the necessary detailed and intimate guidance only to a few chosen disciples. Those who receive only indirect or distant indications from a school cannot go far without danger of losing the vital harmony of the many partial processes within the total process. Man is a most complex being who exists on several levels, each of which is governed by its own laws. These laws, though quite distinct in their operation, are connected with one another. A simple example will show what is meant by the 'laws of different levels'. The activity of the human body is governed by mechanical laws (levers, heat engines, hydrodynamic apparatus), by physico-chemical laws (digestion of food, oxygenation of blood, synthesis of special proteins and amino-acids, etc.), by biological laws (development, regeneration, reproduction) and by psycho-nervous laws (thought, feeling, instinct, etc.). These laws belong to different levels yet they are interdependent and we cannot understand the activity of the organism unless we recognize both their distinctness and their interaction. Besides these, there are also higher laws connected with the attention, with the power of choice and its exercise, with the will and the understanding, and the still higher realms of the soul and its powers. Each and all of these laws is involved in the process of self-perfecting, and if a man seeks to direct this process by his own will and understanding, he needs to know - if not the laws themselves - at least the critical phases of their operation.

Those who believe that it is possible for man's nature to be transformed by self-discipline usually take far too lightly the complications involved in the harmonious development of body, spirit and soul. They may point to the lives of saints and mystics as examples of the attainments possible with little or no knowledge of the laws of the human psyche, but they forget that for one who attains to blessedness or sainthood, there are many thousands who fall by the way. Moreover, the saint is not necessarily a complete man. Some like St. Francis or St. John of the Cross died young, having destroyed the equilibrium of their bodies by excessive austerities. Others were lacking in practical judgment, as we see in St. Bernard of Clairvaux in his direction of the second Crusade. Moreover, the greatest saints must not be regarded as examples of 'working from without' on the contrary, their strength and their guidance came from within and were bestowed upon them through faith. Their lives are truly unfathomable by the ordinary mind of man.

If we confine our attention to all ways of self-perfecting that are either wholly or predominantly working from without, we must conclude that:

1. A school and a teacher is always necessary.

2. Persistent austerities, physical, mental and emotional, are needed over a long period in order to purify the lower nature.

3. It is at the present time hard to find conditions that make such work possible.

4. It can be successful only with comparatively rare people specially gifted for such an undertaking.

These four conclusions have been amply confirmed in my own experience by the observation, over a period of more than thirty-seven years, of many thousands of students who have followed Gurdjieff's system for the Harmonious Development of Man. I am convinced that this system offers the most complete and effectual method of working from without known in the world today, and one moreover that is particularly well suited to the needs of people of western culture. It has attracted men and women of high mental attainment, emotional sensitivity and practical ability - scientists, doctors, writers, artists and successful men of affairs, besides a solid core of 'ordinary' people. All who have persisted in following the discipline, under the guidance of Gurdjieff's own approved instructors, have attained some measure of harmony and a better understanding of life, and few feel that their efforts have been wasted. But, out of many thousands, only a bare handful have achieved any high degree of spiritual development. No defect is to be imputed to Gurdjieff's system on this account. The truth is that any and every form of working from without is beset with hazards and few can hope to surmount them successfully - even with the strongest desire to do so.

Folk-lore and legend, from the old epic of Gilgamesh that speaks to us from the Epoch of the Search, have always contained allegories of the quest for eternal life as being full of perils that only the rare hero is able to survive.

We need to see the present situation clearly if we are to appreciate the change that has to come. We may be certain that the completion of his being and the fulfilment of his destiny is possible for the man who finds the right teacher for him and who brings the necessary gifts of single-mindedness, sincerity and humility; but we must acknowledge that for the majority, even of those who set out resolutely upon the way, only very few can hope to go far by the methods of working from without.

7. The Inner Working

There are seven principal functions or centres in

man: instinctive, motor, emotional, intellectual, sex, higher emotional and higher mental. The first four of these operate in our ordinary states of consciousness; they are essentially instruments for the present life, and they are incapable of giving us true knowledge either of our own destiny or of objective reality. The sex centre occupies an intermediate position in that it can be an instrument of the lower world, but also a means of lifting man into the truly human world in which there is no separation. The two higher centres are the true instruments of the eternal, imperishable 'Man of the Soul'. The first is the instrument whereby man can know his own true nature and everything that concerns his own destiny, and that of all other men with whom he is related. The second instrument gives access to the eternal mysteries; it is conscious of the Objective Reality that is beyond eternity as it is beyond time.

The distinction between lower and higher centres, between temporal instruments for use in this visible world and eternal instruments that can serve in all worlds is vital for the understanding of inner and outer work, and it has been, to me, of the utmost value in my approach to Subud. We can find much to instruct us on the subject in the mystical writers, and especially in the Sermons of Meister Eckhart. "According to the philosopher who is our chief authority upon the soul no human wisdom ever can attain to what the soul is. That requires supernatural wisdom. What the powers of the soul issue from into act, we do not know: about it haply we do know a little, but what the soul is in her ground, no man knows. Any knowledge thereof that may be permitted to us must be supernatural; it must be by grace: God's agent of mercy." It would indeed be sufficient to refer to Eckhart all that has to be written in this section, for he is wholly concerned with 'working from within' and came nearer to expressing the nature of this work than I could ever hope to do.

The starting point can be stated in Eckhart's words: "There is something in the soul, intimate, mysterious, far higher than the soul herself, whence emanate her powers of intellect and will." The lower centres, or ordinary self of man and his lower nature, are cut off from this mysterious 'something'. In it lie sleeping, or more truly, still unborn, all the potentialities of eternal life. The aim of all religion, of all asceticism, of all 'work on oneself', of all the striving of man for perfection, is to reach and awaken this inner 'something'. And this is equally true of working from without and of the working from within, that we are trying now to understand.

In the truest and fullest sense, working from within can start only when the inner 'something' is awakened. There then flows from within a stream of influences that act first upon the higher centres-the instruments of the soul - and from them penetrate into and through the lower centres and the bodily organism. These influences then produce reactions in the lower centres exactly similar to those of intentional self-discipline except that they are not standardized. Each individual is subject to an influence that, having passed through his own higher emotional centre, corresponds exactly to his own needs, and, moreover, to his needs at each stage of his inner development. Thus working from within is analogous to the development of the embryo from the time that the ovum is fertilized. The organism with all its limbs, organs and functions is not imposed from without, but arises under the influence of the genetic pattern with which the child is endowed at the moment of conception. Modern embryologists with their marvellous techniques are still quite unable by 'working from without' to reproduce a thousandth part of the minutely adjusted regulative process by which the embryo develops.

This analogy might seem to suggest that 'working from without' is as useless as the attempt to 'synthesize' a human child in a laboratory. The growth of being must always occur spontaneously from within. Our efforts can create favourable conditions for this growth, but they cannot compel it to occur. We have many obstructions that have accumulated in us - some from our heredity and the influences of our early lives - others the results of our own voluntary or involuntary submission to negative impulses coming from without. We can do much by our own efforts to remove these obstructions so that the life-giving energy can flow freely through all our centres and all our organs. All this is true, but when we try to go further and mould ourselves upon some ideal pattern received from without, we run into the danger of standardization and are liable to find ourselves stretched upon the Procrustean bed without power to rise from it again. This is called by Gurdjieff 'wrong crystallization', and he paints a vivid picture of the plight of those who make the mistake of relying upon their own strength. Right crystallization means the unification of the whole being and nature of man according to his own essential pattern, and it is achieved by a process of development that must be directed from the pattern itself and not from without. But although 'we', that is, our ordinary self, cannot direct the process, we can watch over it and protect the being in us that is later to be born and become the true self or man in us. When working from without is understood in this way, it is more than useful - it is necessary.

The emphasis placed upon the awakening of the soul and the rebirth to which it leads requires also that we should state plainly how the awakening comes about. Here we have all the authority of Scripture and the evidence of the great mystics that it is only the Holy Spirit that awakens the mysterious something that initiates the train of events that I have called 'working from within'. Indeed, as Kant showed in his *Critique of Practical Reason*, it is the awakening of the soul that validates our belief in God and Eternal Life. The central point of all religious experience is the contact between man and God, mediated by the Holy Spirit and made through that mysterious 'something' in the soul that is in neither time nor space, and cannot be said to exist at all until it is awakened.

It seems to me that we come nearest to the truth if we say that the ordinary man has no soul but only the possibility of acquiring one, and that he cannot enter into eternal life unless and until his soul is born. The saying of Christ, "What shall it profit a man if he gain the whole world and lose his own soul?" can only mean that the man who closes himself to the contact with the Spirit of God by attaching himself exclusively to the values of this world loses the opportunity of gaining the soul that is - until it is awakened - a *possibility* and no more.

The phrase: 'working from within' refers to the process that starts in man when his soul is awakened. He is brought thereby into contact with the power of the Holy Spirit - the Lord and Giver of Life. This gift of life streams downwards from the highest point of the man's being and flows through all levels. Because it is a life-giving power it brings to life every part that it reaches. Thus there comes about a true rebirth that is also a resurrection.

In this operation, the only act of will required of us must be that of consent and acceptance. We cannot 'will' the process, nor can we direct or regulate it. It regulates itself by the very fact that the life-force flows through our essence pattern, thereby acting constantly to restore us to ourselves, to enable us to become the real man or the real woman that from the moment of conception we were destined to be.

Although we cannot, from our ordinary self, initiate or direct a process that has its source at an immeasurably higher level of consciousness, it does not follow that we remain unaware of the process or unable to co-operate with it. We experience the working from within as an inner urge or prompting that shows us what we have to do and gives us, moreover, the power to do it. I cannot do better to end this chapter than by quoting Meister Eckhart's final message to his friends. He said: "I will give you a rule which is the sum of all my arguments, the key to the whole theory and practice of the truth.

"It very often happens that a thing seems small to us which is of greater moment in God's sight than what looms large in ours. Wherefore it behoves us to take alike from God everything he sends us without ever thinking or looking to see which is greatest or highest or best but following blindly God's lead, that is to say, our own feeling, our strongest dictates, what we are most prompted to do. Then God gives us the most in the least without fail.

"People often shirk the least and prevent themselves getting the most in the least. They are wrong. God is everywise, the same in every guise to him who can see Him the same. There is much searching of heart as to whether one's promptings come from God or no; but this we can soon tell for if we find ourselves aware of, privy to, God's will above all when we follow our own impulse, our clearest intimations, then we may take it that they come from God."

Herein lies the best assurance for those who are beset by doubts and scruples about following the promptings of conscience, lest that which seems to be the voice of conscience may be the voice of the tempter.

We have come now to the threshold of the Subud experience, and I shall try to show how we may recognize that this is really the awakening of the soul for which we all search.

5. THE LATIHAN

1. *The Meaning of 'Latihan'*

THE Indonesian word *latihan* cannot adequately be translated into English. Its root – *latih* - conveys the notion of becoming familiar with something, to assimilate and take it into oneself. The nearest equivalent is probably *training*. The common translation 'exercise' is misleading in so far as it is associated with the idea of some set form of work such as physical exercise, mental exercise or religious exercise. All these relate to the 'working from without' that is the exact opposite of the latihan. After the initial act of will by which we submit to the process, the training received in the latihan does not come from any intentional action of our own. In the latihan, we are gradually pervaded and permeated with the life force that flows into us from our own awakened soul.

Although latihan is a training of the whole man, it is not undertaken for the sake of the result. Pak Subuh insists that the true meaning of the latihan is worship of God. The training is the result of worship, but it is worship that is essential; the result is incidental. The phrase 'worship of God' requires explanation, especially in these days when so many people have revolted against religion because they imagine that worship is incompatible with any acceptable conception of Deity. They argue that a God who demands worship of His creatures is an anthropomorphic conception; a relic of tribal theology, when God was pictured as a King reigning in the heavens and, in His demands, little different from a human tyrant. "For I the Lord thy God am a jealous God, visiting the iniquity of the fathers upon the children unto the third or fourth generation of them that hate Me." When we read such passages we must remember that they belong to the Hemitheandric Epoch, whose Master Idea was that of human dependence upon Heroic help. With each succeeding lesson, infant humanity has gained a deeper realization of the meaning of Deity. If we no longer entertain such naively anthropomorphic conceptions of the Creator, it does not follow that worship has ceased to have a meaning. It has already long been clear to theologians that God does not demand worship because He needs it or desires it, but because it is the means whereby the soul of man can return to the Source from which it came. It is also well understood that worship is the state or condition in which man stands in the presence of his Creator: it is the recognition or awareness that there is an immense Power that is greater than all other powers, and that this Power is benevolent towards all creatures, including man.

What is not so well understood, even by theologians, is that the state or condition of worship cannot be reached by the temporal instruments of man - that is, by the lower centres. We may with our minds and feelings, and even with our bodies, wish to worship God, but these are merely instruments; they cannot be the worshipper himself. Worship is a power exclusive to the soul of man, for it is only in the soul that there can be a direct consciousness of the Power and Love of God. Worship cannot originate in the mind or the heart, however much we may know with our minds that worship is necessary and feel with our hearts the desire to worship. True worship is the conscious acceptance of the condition we shall be in at the moment of death when our personal will is taken from us.

A simple observation can convince anyone of the truth of this apparently hard saying. Sometimes in the presence of a great natural phenomenon such as a mighty storm at sea or even a great range of mountains white with snow, the sense of our own nothingness in comparison with the powers of nature overwhelms us, and we experience a state of awe that is at the same time filled with peace and thankfulness that such great things should be revealed to us. It is easy to verify that such an experience does not originate in the mind or the feelings, nor is it the result of our own desire to admire or 'worship' nature. If we begin to 'think about' the experience into which we have been lifted, we fall back at once into our ordinary state; likewise, if we begin to enjoy the state, it changes into something personal and false. If earthly nature can lift us to an intensity of experience that is beyond the mind and the feelings, how much more should we expect that worship of God should be a condition entirely beyond the reach of our ordinary functions.

It does not follow that in the latihan the body, feelings and mind have no part to play, but they are the instruments, not the actor. When, and only when, the higher centres are awakened, an action begins in the lower centres that eventually brings them into harmony with the higher centres. This is the 'training' to which the word latihan refers. When all the organs and their functions are trained to be receptive to the fine influences and impulses that proceed from conscience in the depths of the soul, then all participates in worship. True worship comes from the whole man from his highest soul powers to the skin and bone of his body. Worship is training, but it is a training that comes wholly from within.

Religious people tend to assume that, if their minds and feelings are active in worship, then their soul is worshipping also. They refer to mind and feelings as 'powers of the soul' and this leads to the error of supposing that the soul must be awake whenever the powers are exercised. The truth is that whenever worship originates in and is directed by our own will, it can only be worship by and of the instruments, not worship by and of the soul. This is a hard saying, but unless it is understood, the defects of human worship can never be grasped.

2. Approach to Subud

Since we cannot of our own will initiate the 'working from within' of the Subud latihan, the question naturally arises, "What then is the role of our own will, of our own power of choice and of our ability to make efforts?" The answer to this question must be understood by everyone who wishes to approach Subud rightly. We cannot *do* anything, but we can *ask*. To ask is to commit oneself to the results that will follow if we receive what we ask for. Thus, to ask should be a responsible exercise of the freedom of choice that is man's most precious gift. In order to ask responsibly, we should at least know what we are asking for and be able to foresee and understand the consequences of receiving it. But who are 'we' that ask? The ordinary man is not *one*. He exists on various levels, but is aware only of two: that of material objects and that of his thoughts and feelings. On each level, he has different functions that are only loosely connected with one another. He is a multiplicity of selves, a succession of states, a being who does not and cannot know himself. There is no 'I' that rules over the many selves, for the 'I' that should be the ruler lies unborn in the depths of his unawakened essence. Since at any given moment one of the many selves that make up our personality is uppermost, that single self can ask. Later, another self may repudiate the asking, if its needs and wishes lie in quite a different direction. Those who do not understand this, and who trust themselves and believe that whatever they say and do comes from the whole of their being, may not feel the incongruity of asking from some transient, superficial self for the awakening of their innermost soul. Those who have begun to understand their true situation are likely to be very diffident in asking and to doubt whether their power of choice can extend to so momentous a decision.

To protect those who with the impulsiveness of ignorance are ready to ask for what they cannot understand, and to give confidence to those who have realized something of their own limitations, the approach to Subud is made subject to a period of probation. Under special conditions - as in the case of people coming from afar with little time to make the contact - the probation may be reduced to a nominal period of waiting. Nevertheless, the principle is unaffected: it is that one must first ask oneself the question whether one truly wishes to receive, and only after receiving *from oneself* an affirmative answer, to ask *from another* that the contact should be given.

Let us suppose that William Jones enquires about Subud, having read in the papers or heard from friends an account that is almost certainly misleading in many aspects. After sundry attempts he finally receives explanations of the kind given in this book. It is impressed upon him that Subud is not a kind of faith healing nor a system of mental or spiritual exercises. If, after various misunderstandings are cleared away, William still wishes to enter Subud, he places his name on the probation list, which entitles him to put any questions he wishes and to receive answers, even if these involve Subud members in speaking about their own personal experiences in the latihan.

Here it is necessary to explain why such answers can be given freely, whereas it is usually understood that schools possessing knowledge of spiritual methods are very careful in selecting those to whom these methods should be transmitted. Herein lies one cardinal difference between working from without and working from within.

The effect of spiritual exercises should be to break down the crust of illusions and bad habits that separates the personality from the essence. This often requires a powerful action that can be very disturbing to the psyche. Again it is sometimes necessary to awaken a particular function by forcing it to attain - for a time - a high degree of activity. Unless great care is taken this may disturb the working of other functions.

An example of the dangers is provided by breathing exercises. The human organism is so constituted that there is a delicate instinctive balance between the rate of breathing, the speed and volume of the pulse, and the discharge into the blood of hormones and other substances known and still unknown to science. The respiration is also closely related to the rhythms of the brain and nervous system. If the rate and pattern of breathing are intentionally altered, all the other functions connected with it must be adjusted, or harm to the organism will result. But those who teach so-called Pranayama, or the control of breathing practised by Yogis, seldom know about all these connections. Therefore in true Yogi schools - with which, it must be said, western students scarcely ever come in contact - the secrets of Pranayama are carefully guarded. The most powerful exercises are never taught except to specially selected disciples, who must remain under the close supervision of a guru. The same applies to mental and religious exercises. Many a yogi and many a monk has died prematurely or lost his reason through following such exercises without an experienced and responsible guide.

The reason for these precautions becomes evident if we reflect that exercises are standardized, whereas man is not standardized. The only safeguard against the dangers is secrecy, and there is no other motive for secrecy except to protect people from forces that they do not understand and cannot direct.

It is entirely different with 'working from within'. First of all, there can be no imitation, no stealing of ideas and methods before the pupil is ready. Since the work proceeds from within and adapts itself to the needs of each person, there is no need for secrecy; and there is no need for precautions, except to ensure that the seeker abstain from introducing his own ideas and bringing his own wishes, his own will into operation. If he were to do so, he would expose himself to a mixed action that comes partly from his own soul and partly from his self-will, and that would create a danger; but it is not a danger that can be averted by secrecy. On the contrary, the more people know about the experiences of others, the less are they likely to mistake their own self-will for the Will of God. Therefore, in Subud, everyone is free to speak of their own experiences and of what they receive in and from the latihan. Since no one can induce for himself the action of the latihan, whatever may be told remains 'outside'. Nevertheless, it enables those who wish to approach Subud to understand what is needed before they ask to be admitted.

The need can be stated very simply. We ask that we should be put in contact with the Holy Power that gives Life to the soul of man. We recognize that the contact must be made beyond ourselves - not 'beyond' in the sense of outside - but beyond our minds and feelings, in the higher, the eternal part of ourselves. Since we are imprisoned in the lower, temporal part of our nature, we cannot, of our own will, reach the place where the contact is to be made, and therefore we must ask for help. This asking is an act of our own, and we can only make it with that part of us which is aware of what it means. That is, for nearly all people, their personality, since the essence is still asleep. Thus, our asking is inevitably incomplete. The latihan itself is the means whereby the incomplete, imperfect asking can be completed and made perfect.

If all this can be made more or less clear to our William Jones, he sees that he must ask not for results, but for the opening of possibilities. He does not ask because he understands what he wants, but because he realizes that he does not understand.

3. The Opening

It seems to me that the easiest way to understand the 'opening' is to compare it with Christian Baptism. The mystery of baptism is that the child is received into the number of Christ's flock without understanding or even being aware of what is being done for it. Even in adult baptism the mystery remains, for it implies a profound change of the entire nature, of which the person received into baptism can be only dimly aware.

In baptism, the question is put and answered, not by the child but by the godparents who stand as witnesses. They are presumed already to have experienced the inward change that comes from the awakening of the soul's powers, and when they ask for baptism on behalf of the child they bear witness to the truth and reality of the transformation. Unfortunately, baptism, this holy symbol of the Christian faith, has lost nearly all its meaning, so that even sincere Christians do not understand their responsibilities. The very form of the Christian service suggests 'working from without', since the godparents are enjoined to see that the child is taught the Creed and the Commandments, and is brought to the bishop for confirmation. Thus what is, in reality, a matter of faith in the Grace of God is made to appear as a promise to fulfil certain external obligations.

Those who have received the latihan come to understand

from their own experience the meaning of faith and of Grace, and if they belong to the Christian profession, they find that all the Sacraments of their religion acquire a new depth and a new power. If they are called upon to be godparents, they see for themselves that the moment of baptism is indeed a moment of opening, when the Holy Spirit enters and gives birth to the new man.

In Subud the opening is performed without ceremony and without any kind of ritual. The trainees stand - or, if they are aged or infirm, sit - and the man or the woman who is to open them reminds them that they have come because they wish to find the way to the true worship of God.

Many people have asked how the opening is 'done'. The answer is that nothing at all is done, either by those who receive the contact or by those who are witnesses. Faith cannot be transmitted from one person to another. But the 'witness' has been accepted by God as an instrument, and the faith which has been given to him makes the contact possible for the other.

Although the contact itself is made not in time, but in eternity, the latihan itself lasts for half an hour or more. This makes it possible for the inner working to begin, even though most of those who receive the contact are at first aware of nothing at all. When there are physical sensations and movements, or new states of feeling, the newcomer recognizes that 'something' has happened, but the true nature of this something cannot be grasped at all.

When the opening is completed, many trainees enjoy a feeling of deep relaxation and peace, and realize with astonishment that they have been more fully conscious of themselves, for a longer time and in a more continuous state, than is possible by any effort of attention that they are capable of making.

There are a few, very few, whose experience is much stronger and deeper, and who have no doubt from the first that they have been in the presence of a Holy Power. There are also many trainees who at first experience little or nothing and are disappointed that "nothing seems to have happened". To such, patience is advised and persistence, for our practical experience has shown that not one in a hundred who persist with the latihan fails, within two or three months, to become aware of a new force working in him, and sees results that convince him that something has occurred that has not come from his own thought, feeling or desire.

Some experiences of the opening are definitely unfavourable or painful. Some trainees are convinced that there is indeed a force, but an evil one. Others are simply afraid. Others again feel resentful or suspicious, or simply are embarrassed, and do not wish to continue. Those who have seen much of Subud and its action on many people, recognize that these are all reactions of the personality which soon cease to trouble those who can bring themselves to persist. Since everyone, sooner or later, encounters difficulties due to the reactions of the personality, the *act of will* that consists in choosing to continue, has to be repeated. This is indeed important, for it makes it clear that the transformation of man does not take place against his own will or without his consent. Indeed, Subud demonstrates in the most practical manner what St. Augustine and other theologians have taught about Grace and the human will.

4. Helpers

Those trainees who have had enough experience to recognize, if not to understand, the action of the latihan can become 'helpers' to those who are still at the beginning. The role of helpers is very important. It is they who can answer the questions of probationers from their own experience. They can also reassure those who are beset by fears and misgivings in the early stages. Helpers also have a part to play in the latihan itself. They are chosen by Pak Subuh himself or by his appointed representatives, and they are permitted to do the latihan more frequently and to receive explanations that will help them to fulfil their duties.

It is a principle of all true spiritual work that he who has received must repay, but this can be done only by helping one's neighbour. The work of a helper is onerous, for he has to bear the burdens of others. This burden-bearing is not a matter only of giving time and attention to the work, but of being ready to take upon oneself the inner state of other people. The helper is more open and more sensitive than those who are still wholly imprisoned in their personalities and in their physical natures. The latter are in process of throwing out the poisons that have accumulated as a result of their past lives, and these poisons enter - in part at least - into more sensitive people in their vicinity, namely the helpers. This can produce very painful or unpleasant experiences. One of the reasons why the helpers are permitted to do the latihan more often is that they can thereby throw out again, or 'cleanse' themselves of, the impurities or poisons they have picked up.

Those trainees who become helpers are soon aware that Subud is not a short cut to an easy life, but rather the acceptance of a heavy burden. Gurdjieff's famous formula, "self-perfecting by way of conscious labour and intentional suffering", is indeed applicable to Subud. As with many other such formulae, the real meaning of what Gurdjieff taught only becomes apparent when a person experiences for himself the inner working, and sees the true nature of human freedom. He is then liberated from the illusion of 'doing', but understands that it is open to him to accept or reject a burden that no one obliges him to bear. His acceptance of the burden involves him in 'conscious labour and intentional suffering'. The suffering is not of the soul, that is his 'I' or true self, but of the instruments, that is the body, the feelings and the mind. Furthermore, this suffering is necessary for his own purification and completion. It is effectual in this only because it is 'conscious and intentional'; that is, accepted by his own free will. Such suffering is compatible with a deep and enduring happiness. Indeed, those who have been privileged to act as helpers are all agreed that they experience a sense of unfailing joy, that comes from realizing that what they are doing is the best for themselves.

It is essential to distinguish the two parts of the helpers' role. The first is external and ordinary: it concerns practical arrangements, advice, consolation and the bearing of the ordinary burdens of those who are sick, troubled or perplexed. Help, in this sense, is the obligation of every man towards his neighbour, and the only new factor in Subud is the inner guidance that enables the obligation to be fulfilled in a manner that is often beyond our understanding. The second part of the helpers' role is inward and extraordinary. It concerns the spiritual exercises. Pak Subuh has repeatedly emphasized that no one can help another in the worship of God. There is no difference, in the latihan, between the helpers and the newcomers - each submits to the working of the Spirit. Therefore the helper in the exercise must never imagine for one moment that he is helping or can help the others. Everyone needs help, but that help cannot come from man. It can come only by submission to the Will of God. The 'bearing of one another's burdens' is then something spontaneous, it is a gift that is accepted, not an action that is done.

The role of the helpers in the latihan requires that they should be able to preserve their own state of conscious surrender to the inward working of the latihan, while at the same time keeping some contact with what is happening to those around them. This is accomplished, not by letting one's attention flow outwards towards others, but by intensifying one's own surrender. It is by no means easy to find the inner balance between one's own worship and 'concern' (in the Quaker sense) with those about one. One learns in the latihan that the two commandments of Jesus - "Thou shalt love the Lord thy God with all thy heart, and with all thy soul, and with all thy mind" and "Thou shalt love thy neighbour as thyself" - have a very precise and literal meaning. The helpers begin to see that it is in our power to fulfil these commandments providing we do not attempt to 'do' anything from our own will. Those who wish to help their neighbours from their own strength and their own understanding shut themselves off from the very possibility of helping anyone.

5. Openers

The 'contact' was first received by Pak Subuh himself. Later he transmitted it to others. When these in their turn had reached a stage of clear conviction as to the reality of the contact and had been strengthened by the latihan to the point where they could bear the forces involved, they could become in their turn 'openers'.

When Pak Subuh came to England he soon designated a small number of men and women as being qualified to act as openers. As I was one of these, I can give some account of the opening as it is experienced by those who are witness for the newcomer.

Those who come to the latihan often ask, "What is it that Pak Subuh does? Does he pray for us? Or has he a power that he directs towards us?" Some think that some kind of hypnotic influence is at work, or even that it is a form of magic. No one who himself has acted as opener can have any doubt on the matter. We do nothing whatever to the people, or even for them. The opener enters the latihan exactly as if he were alone in the room. Indeed the sense of being alone in the presence of a great Power is the strongest and clearest element of the whole experience. It is that Power that gives new life to the soul, and not ourselves, not anything that we do. Pak Subuh says that the witness must have true faith, but I am bound to say that I, for one, am aware of nothing in myself, not even faith. I can say, however, that I have been aware, without any doubt, of the presence of angels during the latihan.

For a time one may cease to be aware of the presence of the others, but there comes a moment when one is conscious of participating in their experience. One knows when someone is being disturbed by his thoughts or his feelings, or whether he is obstructing the process by trying to do something of his own. Those who feel that they 'ought' to be doing something to co-operate with the process communicate their anxiety to the openers. Sometimes there is a feeling of great heaviness, due to the presence of one or more people who are weighed down by their own personality.

A most extraordinary moment of the latihan comes when one is aware that the contact has been made. It is as though the heat of the human passions is quenched for a moment, and the coating of the personality is pierced so that a new life can begin to flow. One is then aware of the presence of a very fine substance or energy that itself is conscious. It would not be inappropriate to describe this energy as a 'supra-sensible light'. This energy envelopes us all and makes it possible to participate in the inner experience of others.

The burden upon those who open is heavy, for they are bound to absorb some of the passions or poisons that are driven out of a person at the moment that the contact is made. Sometimes one feels ill for several days afterwards. In the case of one man who rashly took upon himself to open more people in a given period of time than Pak Subuh had authorized, several months of ill-health were the penalty he had to pay. This risk places a limit upon the transmission of the contact too fast or too often. Generally the burden is greatly lightened when two or more act as 'witnesses' in the opening. Indeed, Pak Subuh lays down as a general rule that one should open while a second stands beside him to share the burden. Nevertheless, when the need arises, all limitations are swept away. Recently, three hundred and twenty-six men and women were opened in Ceylon within three weeks by one man and one woman with the help of two Cinghalese who had themselves been opened during a brief visit to Coombe Springs.

6. Conditions of the Latihan

The Subud latihan is invariably arranged separately for men and women. Men are opened by men and women by women. Not only are the men's and women's latihan separate, but it is recommended that while the state of openness persists - which may be for one or two hours after the latihan - men and women should as far as possible remain apart. An obvious justification for this rule is that, when open, men and women are in a sensitive state and can readily be influenced by one another. There is a deeper reason connected with the very nature of man. This will be discussed later in the chapter on the completion of man. In effect, it means that in the spiritual life it is necessary to accept a strict discipline in regard to the relations between the sexes, for the very reason that deep and strong forces are aroused when the soul of man is given a new life. These forces are necessary, but they cannot be regulated by the human personality. They belong to the essence, and only an awakened essence can direct them aright.

The latihan can be made at any time, but usually not more than thrice a week in the early stages. Some twelve to twenty sessions are usually required before the process is well established. There are, however, great differences between individuals, some receiving almost at once, others requiring many months or even years to become conscious that a new force is working in them.

It is most important that trainees' should understand that they are completely free in the latihan. It begins in them because they ask for it, and it stops when they ask it to stop. Moreover, there is never any loss of consciousness or of the power of choice. It is only when the trainees try to play tricks with the latihan, whether by forcing the pace, by imitating others, or by thinking that they already understand what is still a mystery for them, that they can bring trouble on themselves. Whoever enters the latihan and continues with patience and sincerity, experiences no disturbance. Nevertheless, as I said previously, many trainees imagine that they are being acted upon by Pak Subuh or whoever may open them, that they are being hypnotized or that they are the victims of hallucination. Such notions can easily be dispelled by the simple test that any trainee can apply of seeing whether or not he is free at any moment he chooses to stop the latihan and walk out of the room. Still more cogent for those who understand something of the meaning of will and consciousness, is the observation that one remains at all times fully conscious of oneself - even if one ceases to be aware of one's surroundings. Since one effect of the latihan is to bring to the surface of one's consciousness states of mind usually buried in the subconsciousness, people with hidden fears find themselves afraid, those with concealed suspicions become overtly suspicious, those rooted in self-concern become obsessed with the idea that they are doing better or receiving more than they are. All such effects create problems and embarrassments and put people in need of help from those with greater experience.

Usually, after a few months, such difficulties have been overcome and trainees understand clearly that their freedom of choice is never for a moment removed from them and that there is no danger at any time of losing consciousness. They also become convinced that the action in the latihan comes from within themselves, and not from any other person. When this stage is reached, people are authorized to continue the latihan alone in their own homes. Usually, they can then become helpers for others.

In this chapter, I have described the latihan, but not its effects. In later chapters, I shall give examples of the manner in which the latihan works in people of different types and conditions. There is no 'normal' latihan. This is disconcerting for those who are accustomed to base their judgments on comparisons with some accepted standard or norm. They want to ask the question: "Am I getting on better or worse than the others?" But this question, which is intelligible as applied to working from without, has no meaning when we enter the process of working from within. Since there are no standards, there can be no comparisons; since there is no time, there can be no 'rate of progress'. Each trainee is what he is, and his inner development must follow his own laws. The uniqueness of the human soul is part of its dignity, and those who seek for comparisons or external tests of their progress belittle the soul as much as those who imagine that it can be changed against its will.

6. THE SUBUD EMBLEM

1. Susila Budhi Dharma

THE word *Subud* is a contraction of three words - Susila Budhi Dharma. The ancient Sanskrit language from which these words are taken belongs to the Hemitheandric Epoch, and has not been a spoken tongue for nearly three thousand years. Nearly all the wisdom of the old Epochs has been lost, and we do not understand much of the symbolism of the Vedas and Brahmanas. Yet the three words Susila – Budhi - Dharma convey a deep and vivid meaning as they are interpreted by Pak Subuh.

Susila means literally to have good morals. Pak Subuh describes it as "Right living according to the Will of God".

The word Budhi has baffled the commentators. Some understand by it the Power of the Intellect, others Consciousness, and others again explain it as the inner agent, or will of man. Pak Subuh takes it to mean "The inner force or power that resides within the nature of man himself". It is not the individuality or self-hood of man, nor even his soul, but rather the limitless potentiality for development and progress that is the true motive power in the spiritual life.

Few Sanskrit words have been so misused as Dharma. In the motto of the Theosophical Society - *Nasti Satyat para Dharmo* - it is translated as religion. It is often taken to mean law, or the world order. Others again translate it as duty or even fate. The Pali equivalent, Dhamma, occurs in one of the most ancient Buddhist scriptures - the Dhammapada - as the description of the way of life of the Bhikkhu or Buddhist mendicant priest. Pak Subuh interprets Dharma to mean "Submission, surrender and sincerity in receiving the gift of Grace from the Almighty".

When the three words are combined, they denote the perfect harmony of the inner life {Budhi) and outer life (Susila) that is attained when our entire being is submitted to the Will of God as it is revealed to us through the highest centre of consciousness, seated not in the brain but in the soul.

Subud is a way of life. It is neither a dogma nor a creed nor is it a teaching nor a philosophy. It presupposes an act of faith; namely the acceptance of the possibility that the Will of God can be revealed to the individual man or woman whose soul is brought to life and whose lower instruments of thought and feeling have been purified. It does not require that the act of faith should precede the awakening, but only that one should be ready to enter upon a path the end of which may be the complete transformation of one's inner and outer life. Subud means not merely to live rightly, which would apply equally to living according to the commandments we receive from without. It means to live rightly *from within*, by the Will of God and by His Grace. We have obligations here on earth - represented by the word Susila - and we have the power so to fulfil them that we do not offend against Divine Ordinance. This is the way that leads to felicity not only in this life, but in the life to come. The way is limitless, for it is the path of return to the Infinite.

This suggests a second and deeper meaning for the word Subud. Pak Subuh has explained that it should also be taken as a reminder of the great universal law: "Everything that arises from a Source must return again to its Source" or "That which proceeds from God returns to God again".

2. The Subud Emblem

Seven golden circles transected by seven radial lines is the emblem of Subud. The circle has always been regarded as the symbol of endlessness, for it has no stopping point. The circle as a symbol means that belief in the possibility of unlimited development, endless progress of the human soul. The seven circles indicate that this development implies different levels, and that within each level there is a source out of which all proceeds and into which it returns. The seven radial lines indicate that the qualities of all levels are reproduced on each level. There are thus seven levels and seven qualities, making forty-nine different states, stages or conditions.

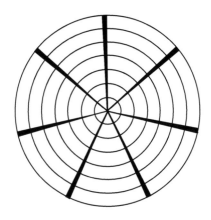

3. The Seven Soul Powers

The seven circles represent the seven great spheres of universal life, and they also signify the seven modes in which this life is manifested.

These can be described as souls or powers. It is always hard to find a suitable word to describe the quality that characterizes a particular class of essences. The soul itself cannot be separated from its own qualities, nor can the qualities be found elsewhere than in the kind of soul to which they belong. Nevertheless, it seems best to use the word power to designate the seven modes of existence which influence human life. They are:

7 The Power of the Supreme Lord.
6 The Power of Compassion.
5 The Power of the Complete Man.
4 The Human Power.
3 The Animal Power.
2 The Vegetative Power.
1 The Material Power.

Only the four lowest of these seven are accessible to the mind of man and can, therefore, be described by means of words and images. The three highest levels are entirely beyond the apprehension of the human mind, the fifth and sixth are accessible to the two higher centres in man, but the seventh is beyond the highest possible human consciousness.

We cannot have a right attitude towards Subud unless we grasp one very simple truth. The human mind cannot know anything except what reaches it through the human senses: sight, touch, hearing and the rest. The scholastic philosophers used to say: *there is nought in the mind that was not first in the senses.* This truth is accepted today, as it has always been by anyone who takes the trouble to examine what our thoughts are made of. It does not, however, follow that there is no reality that our senses cannot perceive. On the contrary, we can see only a small part, and hear and touch a small part of what is actually around us. Our minds cannot know this, because they really are limited by our senses. So that although we may talk and write about an invisible world, about eternal realities, about life after death, about the soul and conscience and even about God - we cannot know anything at all about these supra-sensible objects. Neither can anyone else know them. Our minds are shut in by a barrier through which thought cannot pass. But we are not the same as our minds, any more than we are our head or our hands. All these are instruments of man, not the man himself.

We could not even suspect the existence of powers higher than our human powers, if there were not in us instruments that are themselves higher than the mind. But, just because these instruments are indeed higher, they cannot be brought under the control or expected to obey the orders of the mind. They will obey the soul, whose instruments they are, but if the soul is asleep or unborn, then they have no master, and they must remain suspended until the master comes.

All that can be said about the three highest powers is that they do not arise and grow out of the lower ones, as plants grow from minerals, animals from plants and man from animals. The power of the complete man enters him from above - it is a gift that depends solely on the Grace of God. Only when the human soul is filled with this power can it reach perfection and enter the realm of the just man made perfect that is beyond anything that our senses can ever perceive.

The sixth power is far higher and greater than that of the complete or perfect man. It is universal - not confined within the limits of our solar system. The soul that is illuminated by this sixth power participates in the Divine Compassion by which all worlds are sustained.

Of the seventh power we can say nothing at all. It seems that it must arise from beyond the whole existing universe - but these are mere words. We cannot even know what we mean by the 'Power of God'. The soul into which this Power enters is wholly united in its Will with the Will of God. But since the soul itself is a creature and can never be the same as God, we cannot hope to understand this unity of Will, unless God himself chooses to reveal it to us.

Even if description is useless, there is a value in setting before ourselves the names of the Higher Powers, if only so that we can remember that human nature, even when raised to its highest level of perfection, is still two degrees removed from the Power of the Supreme Lord.

4. The Lower Powers

Since in every man one of the four lower powers is predominant, it is important that we should understand their nature. The mind of man cannot penetrate to the inward essence, even of these lower powers, because we are able to think only about the external, visible forms. The inward essence cannot be represented by means of images. We can, however, learn to recognize the working of the different powers, and so become sensitive to their qualities as they are manifested in ourselves.

The first of the essential powers is that which works through material objects. It is this power that acts upon our senses and enables us to see and touch and form images. The words we use in speaking and thinking acquire their meaning from these sense images. Thus when we say the word 'table', we evoke in ourselves the forces that act on us when we see and touch a table, and so we have an image of a table. We have the same kind of images when we say 'tree' or 'cow' or 'man'. This means that all our images belong to the power of material objects.

We cannot doubt that there is such a power, because material objects are able to attract our attention and arouse our interests and our desires. Nevertheless, this power belongs to the lowest world, and for this reason it is also called the satanic power. Those whose souls are dominated by the power of material objects feel themselves secure only when they have possessions around them. They are afraid of losing their possessions because their soul can find no other support. Men will even kill themselves if they lose their possessions, and they will kill or harm others in order to acquire them. Even if they are restrained from such violent actions, by training or habit or fear, they are nevertheless dependent on material things, and value themselves and others by the quantity and quality of the possessions they can collect round them. Such people cannot even imagine that they are the slaves of the satanic power, because they have no other experience with which to compare their own.

It is a hard saying, but true, that nearly all people in the world today live under the power of material objects and cannot exist without them. The satanic power also dominates the earth itself - that is the material planet with its earth, water and air. Therefore people who are under the material power are imprisoned on the earth. They can exist only on the earth, and when they die their only possibility of further existence is to return to the earth. If, however, the soul is not brought to life, the essence cannot easily find its way back into a human form, and is likely to be absorbed into the material objects to which it is so much attached.

The second power is that of the plant essence. This power is far more highly differentiated and more 'alive' than the material power. It is the support of all life on the earth, not merely in the form of food for our bodies, but as the source of all the diverse impulses that form the 'nature' of men and animals. For this reason the vegetative power is sometimes called also the *force of desire*. Those who are dominated by this power are clear and strong in their impulses.

The 'world of plants' is far higher than the world of material objects. It is an invisible world, for it is composed of the essences that are hidden in the plants. To understand this we must refer again to the Subud emblem, and remember the seven lines that transect the seven circles. Thus a man may be under the influence of plant powers and yet be able to perceive only that which reaches him through his senses. Then he sees plants only as material objects and has no respect for the essences that are hidden in them.

The third power, that of the animal forces, is the source of the 'character'. Thus, some men have the character of a dog, others of a bull or a pig or a tiger. These 'characters' are hidden by the external human form and by the outer human instruments, especially the mind; that is, all that I have called the 'personality'. Consequently, we do not easily recognize the essential characters of people, and suppose that all 'men' are really men. The quality of the essence depends upon the powers that predominate in it. Thus it is possible for a 'man' to have the character of a dog and to be dominated by material or satanic influences, and yet he and other people take for granted that he really is a man. Many such strange combinations are possible, and when we begin to acquire the faculty of perceiving the hidden realities, we understand that 'humanity' is still very far from being truly human.

The comparison of mankind to a child is far from adequate for it does not allow for the immense complexity of the whole human situation. In one aspect, humanity can be compared to a child of four or five years old. In another, we must think of the slow emergence from the animal essence into the human essence that started a bare million years ago, and may take several more millions of years to complete. Our human organs and functions are subject to predominantly sub-human powers in our nature. Again, mankind is an integral part of the entire life of the earth - the biosphere - and can never be understood apart from this whole to which we all belong. In this respect, the entire human race is rather more in the situation of an embryo still contained and nourished in the womb, than a child already born and in some measure competent to see to its own needs. Thus, the influence upon men of the animal power is more important and penetrates more deeply into our nature than those of the material and vegetative powers. In the Megalanthropic Epoch, with its emphasis upon the salvation of the individual, the *organic* significance of mankind - of the whole human race - was almost lost to sight. It is a clear indication of the coming of the new Epoch that men are turning more and more towards the realization of human solidarity and interdependence. We may expect that during the next two or three thousand years humanity will come to the consciousness of its own unity with the rest of life upon the earth. Then people will begin to be aware of the immense significance of the animal essence and the power that flows through it.

The fourth or human power is that which flows through the human essence. Inasmuch as mankind has not yet evolved to the stage at which there is a true social consciousness, the mutual influence of human beings upon one another very seldom comes from the human power. Nearly always the action either proceeds from the lower powers, and especially those of the material world, or else it comes from the personality, that is, the artificial covering by which the essence is enveloped. The true brotherhood of mankind must come from the operation of the human power - but so long as men are closed up by their personality and subject even in their essence to sub-human forces, there can be no 'brotherhood from within'. Consequently the social relationships of mankind as we know them today are almost exclusively the result of external attractions and outward restraints.

We must not blame people for this situation. It is inevitable in our present immature state, and thousands of years may have to pass before a truly human society can arise on the earth and embrace all organic life within a single family. Nevertheless, we can already see in the working of Subud that those who can persist through the early stages come to a new and essential realization of what a human society should be, and can begin to experience the working of the human power in their relations with their fellow men.

Although nearly all the wealth of experience that enters through the human power is closed to those whose soul is not yet brought to life, there is one manifestation that is necessary for human existence and is therefore made to operate independently of the inner condition. This is the power of sex. The relationship between man and woman is a true human relationship that penetrates through the personality and acts in the essence. Consequently, the relationship of the sexes, at all times and for all people, has provided the greatest opportunities and has also been fraught with the greatest hazards for the human soul. Pak Subuh reminds us that the sexual force is the very first to enter man's life, since it is present at the moment of conception. The Subud Emblem reminds us that every power cuts through all levels, and it can therefore happen that a high power in the soul comes under the domination of a lower power in the essence.

This is indeed what almost always happens with the power of sex: in nearly all men and women it is directed by the animal powers, influenced by the vegetative passions and brought to shame by the material or satanic powers. When the human power is rightly manifested in the human essence, it is the means for the completion of man and for his preparation for the Divine Grace of the perfected human soul.

5. The Two Universal Essences

There is in the Subud Emblem an invisible as well as a visible content. We are shown in the seven circles and the seven rays how the seven qualities appear in each of the seven levels, but not how it is possible to pass from one level to another, nor how all are united into a single whole. The emblem is completed by the addition of two further essences that cannot be shown by points or lines or circles or any other geometrical symbol, for they are omnipresent, pervading all that exists. These are the Primal Essence, and the Holy Essence, or Holy Spirit.

The Primal Essence is also called the Great Life Force that flows through everything from the highest to the lowest, and from the lowest to the highest. It is called by Gurdjieff the "common-cosmic-Ansanbaluiazar", which he defines by the formula "Everything issuing from everything and again returning into everything".[1] The flow of the Primal Essence from above below and from below above is called Involution and Evolution, and it is responsible for the common cosmic exchange of substances by which the life of the entire universe is maintained.

The Sacred Essence that proceeds directly from the Will of God, and surrounds and pervades everything, is the Power that makes possible the return of all essences to their source. Thus in the Creed it is also called The Lord and Giver of Life.

It would be useless even to attempt an analysis of the innumerable ways in which the two Universal Sacred Essences have been described in the scriptures of all religions, as well as in the hermetic books of all ancient schools. There is no new teaching in Subud and it is unnecessary to spend more time in seeking for parallels.

Although names can be given to the Sacred Essences and even some kind of description of the characteristics can be attempted, the truth is that, being limitless and omnipresent, it is quite impossible for the limited, localized human functions of thought, feeling and imagination to form any picture of their true nature. Nevertheless, we can recognize their working in ourselves, and especially in the latihan, for it is the Great Life Force that flows through the entire being to give it new life

---

1   *All and Everything*, p. 761.

and new powers. It is the Holy Spirit whose contact awakens the soul and enables it to conform to the Will of God. As the Apostle says: "For it is God which worketh in you both to will and to do of His good pleasure".

Thus, although the Sacred Essences and their Powers are utterly beyond our understanding, they are not remote from us. On the contrary, our very existence and all our potentialities depend upon them alone. Without them, the whole universe and all its content would collapse into nonentity and chaos.

7. THE RESURRECTION
OF THE BODY

1. *First Effects of the* Latihan

AFTER the first few latihan, most trainees report that they observe a sense of deep relaxation and well-being. Both during and after the latihan, they experience an exceptionally clear state of consciousness that persists for one or two hours. These effects are very different from those obtained in voluntary relaxation exercises, which usually produce drowsiness and contentment rather than a state, of vivid consciousness. Again, many trainees report that although they may arrive at the latihan tired and out of temper, they invariably experience a reversal of state and leave the room fresh and cheerful. Such results are to be expected from mild physical exercises that can restore a normal blood circulation after a prolonged period of mental effort, or other sedentary work. Nevertheless, there is a quality that distinguishes the latihan from relaxation exercises and gymnastics, and also from breathing exercises or the use of special postures such as those practised in Hatha Yoga. This quality consists in the *progressive* character of the latihan. So long as the process is not interfered with by any effort of attention, expectation of results or anxiety of any kind, the latihan progressively changes its action, as if some inner energy were opening for itself ever new channels through which to flow. Trainees often show surprise at the sense of novelty and unexpectedness that accompanies almost every latihan. This is characteristic of 'working from within', which reproduces in the outer parts of the self the changes that are taking place in the essence.

One difficulty that was encountered at first by many trainees, but now is gradually disappearing, is in understanding what is meant by 'not thinking'. The effort to exclude thoughts is no different from the effort to keep attention upon a single idea or image. The psychological experiment "How long can you not think about a white elephant?" illustrates the point. So long as one tries to keep the image or thought of a white elephant out of one's attention, it constantly recurs. If one ceases to try, the image soon disappears - we 'forget about it'. Thus all that commonly passes for 'meditation' and 'concentration' is a form of exclusion and is really negative. It closes the channels through which influences of the higher centres should flow. Only in rare cases is true meditation as a prolonged state of complete openness and freedom ever attained, even by those who devote their lives to the practice.

With the latihan, exclusion of any kind is a barrier. Those who try to hold their thoughts upon any idea - even that of worship - obstruct the exercise. Since the inner force is present from the moment of opening, such an effort is a 'kick against the pricks', and those trainees who make it, often complain that the day after the latihan they feel ill or exhausted. These complaints are an indication that the advice 'not to think' has been misunderstood. Such effects in the latihan are mainly responsible for the negative reactions of about one in ten of those who are opened.

The preliminary stage of the latihan may last from one to six months. During this time the effects are mostly transient, and the trainees experience chiefly a sense of well-being that is due to an improvement in the instinctive bodily functions. Even where there are strong emotional reactions, these are usually due, when positive, to the release of tensions in the organism, and when negative, to the resistance of some bodily habit to the inward Power. Pak Subuh has compared this stage to that of a child's first visit to a kindergarten where it is shown the various implements and toys - but has not begun to use them. In order to understand the further process a little better, it is necessary to return to the theme of the last chapter.

2. The Great Life Force

The Primal Essence is the vivifying power by which all existence is sustained. It is the link between the powers of the seven levels of Being. All creation is pervaded by three powers or 'Cosmic Impulses'.[1] These in the Subud terminology are:

The Seven Powers that together make the totality of all *Existence.*

The Great Life Force that is the *Essence* of all essences.

The Holy Spirit that is the *Power of God* enveloping the world.

The Subud contact is made by the Holy Spirit that descends upon the soul of man who is opened to receive it. When the soul is opened, it becomes a receptacle or a channel for the great life force. Through this force, an action is initiated that brings to life all parts of man on all levels, and brings him eventually to the true human soul.

Since there are four lower powers, there are four stages of purification or preparation. These can be represented by the diagram on p. 125.

In the diagram, the four circles represent the four lower powers: material, vegetative, animal and human. They also stand for the physical organism, the feelings or passions, the understanding or intellect, and the true self of man, or consciousness. The four circles are also described as four 'bodies', but these must be understood as essences. Thus the material body is not the same as the physical organism, but is the life force that regenerates the organism and is the seat of the true bodily consciousness or sensation.

The point in the centre represents the Spirit, which is the point of contact at which the Great Life Force enters.

In the latihan, channels are opened by which the life force or life-giving energy flows from the spirit into the physical organism, and regenerates or 'reconnects' it. It is the beginning of this regeneration that is experienced by a trainee as a sense of relaxation, accompanied by a vivid consciousness of being 'present' in his body.

---

1   Cosmic Impulse is the term I have adopted in The *Dramatic Universe,* Vol. II, and which I propose to retain for the purposes of my own personal exposition.

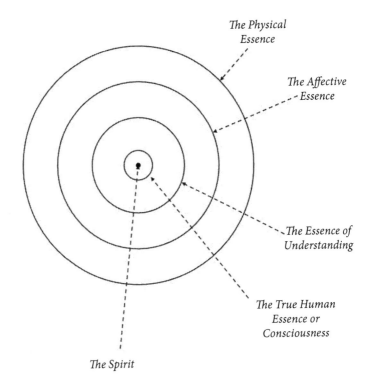

The Physical
Essence

The Affective
Essence

The Essence of
Understanding

The True Human
Essence or
Consciousness

The Spirit

The Four Powers of Man

The life force is unable to flow freely through the organism
so long as there are diseased conditions. These vary from recognized pathological states to hidden tensions and trivial physical
habits. The life force releases the tensions and so produces the
spontaneous movements that occur in the *latihan*. Herein lie the
value and power of 'working from within'. The trainee himself
could not possibly know the movements that he requires-on
the contrary, they are movements that he would usually avoid -
just because of the tensions that they release. Often movements

116

deliberately made to release tensions are very painful, for example, when nerves are affected as in sciatica, or in the many forms of rheumatism and arthritis, where the tensions affect not only the nerves, but also the blood circulation and the activity of the lymph glands. Very often it is observed in the *latihan* that trainees suffering from such complaints make movements that would be agonisingly painful if produced intentionally by force, and afterwards report that they had felt no pain at all.

Not all the movements in the *latihan* are externally visible. Sometimes they are felt like an inner vibration accompanied by a strong sensation of one or other limb or organ. Often again they are so fine as to be unobserved even by the trainee himself. The whole process is one of cleansing of the organism so that the life force can enter. This leads to a general state of bodily health.

When the first 'essence-body' begins to take shape in man, his physical organism is brought to life. This also means that it becomes 'his' own body. So long as the life force has not entered it, the body has no contact with the spirit. It has no master, and the master - that is, the spirit - has no body. This is a strange saying that cannot readily be understood with the mind. But the Subud trainee comes to recognize the truth of it. He realizes that his hands, his eyes, and all his limbs and organs do not belong to 'him' except when the life force is present in him. It can make its home in him only when the body is purified of its defects.

Since the purification proceeds by stages, it can happen that a trainee starts by discovering that one of his limbs or organs has come to life. He recognizes that it is 'his own' in a real sense, the very possibility of which he had never previously imagined. When the process is complete, then the essence-body fills the physical body with life and brings it into submission to the spirit.

This is the true meaning of the resurrection of the body and of the words of the Apostle: "it is raised a spiritual body .... " The resurrection of the body must be completed in this

117

temporal life, if it is to be an eternal reality. This is the first stage of the 'completion' of man.

The second stage is the purification of the feelings, symbolized in the diagram by the arrow that goes from the first to the second circle. To this and the succeeding stages, we shall return in the next chapter.

3. The Latihan and the Body

The first and most obvious change produced by the latihan is an increase in physical energy and the ability to do work. When Subud first came to Coombe Springs, heavy new burdens were placed on an already overworked household. A small number of men - resident students of the Institute - had set themselves to complete the New Hall several months ahead of schedule to make it available for the latihan. Visitors began to arrive from all parts of the world, and all required help which no one was qualified to give them. Moreover, in place of regular study groups held on Saturdays and Sundays with relatively quiet evenings during the week, two or three hundred people were arriving nearly every night for the latihan and turning the house upside down. Under such conditions one might have expected frayed tempers and physical collapse. In the event, not only was the burden carried, but there was an all-round improvement in health and vigour, and the house became quieter than ever before, notwithstanding the avalanche of trainees that descended upon it five nights in the week.

Very soon trainees began to report, with some surprise and diffidence, that they were observing that various complaints had disappeared. Often these were minor chronic conditions of the kind that people get used to without ceasing to be troubled by them. Since the symptoms usually come and go, it is not at once obvious that they have disappeared for good. It was, therefore, not for several months that it became certain that permanent improvements in health had occurred to at least a hundred of the trainees. Typical conditions cured in this way include various skin troubles, colitis, gout, haemorrhoids, lumbago, migraines and insomnia. Only the person concerned can be really sure that something has changed, and people are often inclined to be over hasty in reporting an improvement. Nevertheless, after some sixteen months, it is no longer to be doubted that there has been a noticeable improvement in health among the trainees.

There is something much more telling than all these reports, and that is the quite obvious change in appearance that comes when people are really opened. The impression made upon Mary Cornelius after seven years has already been reported. It happens constantly that people are startled to see a friend's face looking years younger and more beautiful after the latihan. Not only do the trainees themselves feel younger and full of energy, but they are seen by their friends to be so. The presence of the Great Life Force makes itself visibly apparent. The body that is rejuvenated from within acquires a finer texture of complexion and more harmonious movements and gestures.

Nevertheless, it must not be thought that everything is plain sailing. From the first, we observed that some of the trainees began to make very violent movements and to give vent to loud, harsh sounds. The forms of sounds and movements fall into a limited number of classes, from observation of which we have learned to recognize various traits of character that are being eliminated or purified. The purification itself requires that what is inside should come outside. The results can be very disconcerting. A mild, reserved person becomes for a time aggressive and even violent. Tendencies towards jealousy, fear, worry, inner criticism of others, self-importance and the like leave their traces in the physical organism. When the life force enters, these tendencies are driven to the surface, and the overt behaviour is at once affected. In consequence of all this, we have had many difficult moments - especially when a hundred or more people were passing through similar crises. Such crises are usually of short duration, and once they are understood no one is disturbed by them.

119

The same applies to the crises that occur in sick people. In the course of eliminating the poisons, their symptoms are sometimes aggravated. When this occurs it is a good indication that the latihan is working in the organism. Even with people who are not sick, latent traces of old illnesses are soon brought to the surface. I myself within the first three months (January to March 1957) twice passed through two or three unpleasant days when symptoms of dysentery and tuberculosis flared up in me. I suffered a severe attack of dysentery in 1919, and contracted tuberculosis in 1935: though both had been 'cured' I had always been aware that I had weak spots in consequence. After the two crises (about three weeks apart), I felt sure that the last traces of these old illnesses had been eliminated. Later, I had positive evidence that this had in fact occurred. This helped me to give confidence to others who were disconcerted to find they had to 'get worse before they got better'.

Subud is not easy to understand, because we are not accustomed to 'working from within'. Most human activity consists in trying to 'do' something to get what one wants. If the results are contrary to expectation, we either give up or try again. We work 'from the outside upon the outside'. Unavoidably, we overlook many factors, and some we could not discover if we tried, because they are in the 'invisible' world. This is why human 'doing' is so hazardous. When the working is from within, there is no 'doing' - but we have to adapt ourselves to the results. This is possible, for we can see the results and we can (if we have been trained to do so) also see ourselves. Therefore working from within is really much less uncertain and hazardous than working from outside. The most difficult part - the adjustment of the visible process to the invisible pattern - is done for us.

The situation just described may seem strange and even fantastic, and yet we can confirm from our own experience that it is possible to live so that we adapt ourselves to *results* and do not waste our time trying to create *causes* that are beyond our power to control.

A very simple example is the treatment of diabetes. Some people cannot regulate their sugar metabolism. They must either avoid carbohydrates, or take insulin injections, or both. Doctors know the facts, and can keep people in normal health for many years, but medical science does not know the causes of diabetes, beyond the observation that it tends to attack people of a particular temperament, and is aggravated by emotional disturbances. Diabetes is probably due to a psychic injury, and the effects on the body are secondary; there are therefore many ways in which diabetes can be contracted. Doctors do not know how to deal with the psychic injury, and therefore regard diabetes as 'incurable'. They can only alleviate the symptoms by regulating the sugar metabolism.

In the latihan, the psychic injury itself is healed. We have observed numerous cases of diabetics who after starting the latihan have been able progressively to reduce their insulin doses. The improvement has continued over a period of months. I am told that diabetes is prevalent in the overcrowded city of Djakarta, the capital of Indonesia, and that several cases of complete cure have been observed. Patients have not only discontinued insulin but ceased to need to limit their sugar intake. This illustrates what I mean by 'dealing with results' and not attempting to create or destroy causes.

4 The Hidden Forces in Man

The Subud Latihan works deeply in all parts of man's nature. The manifestations which result from its action are sometimes disconcerting and even alarming to those who witness them for the first time.

It is necessary to face the issue squarely. If the inner, or animal, forces in man are not subdued to the true human soul, they can be violent, destructive, lustful or grotesque. We may wish to deny the presence of such sub-human impulses in the average man and regard their appearance among people as evidence of a permanent abnormality or passing psychosis. The facts, however, do not justify the comforting belief that

121

we are not as other men are. All human beings who have not passed through a process of deep purification are tainted with sub-human forces of which they are only partly conscious and which they usually wish to ignore.

One person differs greatly from another in the nature and quality of the sub-human forces present. With a minority - perhaps twenty per cent of all those opened - there is a period of very violent action. This may last a few days to a year or more, during which time the latihan is accompanied by strong bodily movements and loud sounds are produced. These sounds may resemble animals' grunts and cries, or they may be like people in mental agony, or again, they may be like uncontrollable laughter or joyful shouting. Such manifestations are disconcerting to those who have little experience of Subud and have not realized for themselves the strength of the sub-human forces hidden in a man's body. Those who do realize this can also understand that unless these forces come out of a man, he cannot be helped and his true human soul must inevitably languish in helpless passivity. The usurping force must be driven out before the human master can resume his rightful place in us.

Unfortunately most people are convinced that they are already truly and fully human and are indignant or frightened when they are warned that sub-human forces will be aroused in them and will require to be put in their right place.

The true situation can best be described by reference to a conversation which I had recently with a well-known American war-correspondent and writer. During my absence from England he was opened at Coombe Springs. He had declined to come a second time and a mutual friend asked me, when I returned, to see him and perhaps resolve his doubts.

He told me that he had been amazed and horrified by his experience. It seems that on the evening he was opened, owing to some confusion in the arrangements, twenty or thirty men of the 'O' group had come into the hall after about ten minutes and started their exercise. Here it should be explained, that it has been found better to separate the men passing through a period when the action of the exercise is particularly strong in respect of movements and sounds, and to let them exercise together as a special group called 'O' group.

Mr. A. said to me, "I had been asked to keep my eyes closed, but this was quite impossible, and when I looked, I saw men contorting themselves and shrieking as if they were possessed. A picture returned to me, that I cannot bear to remember, of Bucharest after the German withdrawal, when I saw Rumanians pouring petrol over men and women, setting fire to them and dancing like maniacs round the burning bodies. It seemed to me that I was seeing the same evil forces at work. If that is Subud I want no part of it. I prefer the gentility of Jesus, and I believe that religion means love-not madness."

I answered, "Do you really believe that Jesus was genteel? Have you not read in the Gospels how men and women acted when they felt the Power that was in Jesus, how they fell on the ground writhing and screaming? Have you not asked yourself whether in those days Palestine was full of maniacs or wild beasts? To me the picture is unmistakable - in all men there are subhuman forces which are imprisoned in the whitened sepulchres of good manners, training and, perhaps most of all, the fear of public opinion. You have been a war correspondent and you have seen how men, and women too, behave when the outward restraints are removed. I also have been in more than one revolution and I have seen three wars. I have seen racial riots, and only a few weeks ago I was in Ceylon and saw how Buddhists - taught from childhood to abhor violence - had burned down Tamil villages and beaten up and murdered their fellow country-men. Surely you, if anyone, must know what so-called 'human nature' is really like. Do you suppose that we English and Americans are at bottom different from the Rumanians or Germans or the mild Cinghalese? No, we are all alike - it is only the mask that is put on us by education and fastened by fear and training that controls our behaviour. Can you doubt that the present critical situation of humanity all over the world is due to the working of the hidden sub-human forces that paralyse the true human spirit of love and charity?

"If what I say is true - and you know it to be true - then the only possible way in which the future can be saved is by an action deep enough and strong enough to tame the sub-human forces and bring them into submission to the true human forces. I am sure that this is what happened in Palestine two thousand years ago, and it is the same happening again in Subud.

"I do not ask you to believe what I tell you about the purifying action of the Subud latihan; but I do beg you to reflect and ask yourself whether the world can be saved by gentility or whether just such an action as you have seen may not be indispensably necessary. Violent and destructive animal forces are not our only dangers: egoism, cowardice and lust are also perverted manifestations of the animal forces, and all of these must be purged out of us before our true human souls can gain the ascendancy and create on earth a society that can withstand and make right use of the material power that we have acquired through the progress of science, invention, technology and large scale organisation."

Mr. A. was silent, and then said, "Yes, you are right. It is terrible, but it is true. Will you let me come again and try the latihan?" He did come, and afterwards told me that he believed that in Subud there was at least the possibility of a radical and permanent change in the human situation.

Not many weeks after this, England was startled and shocked by the so-called racial disturbances in Nottingham and Notting Hill. Such events are too easily dismissed as the consequences of a bad environment, of faulty education, of economic pressure, of sexual jealousy and so on. The truth is that they are like the smoke that shows that a live volcano is smouldering deep in the earth. The eruption of the volcano cannot be arrested by putting a fence round the crater nor can the animal forces in man be quelled by external restraint. Man can be changed only from within, and, moreover, from so deep a place within himself that the sub-human forces can become aware of the inner master and resume their true status as subordinate powers, that is, as servants and instruments of the human soul. If we do not like the remedy, we should ask ourselves if we prefer the disease. But we had best not pretend that mankind is in a state of sound spiritual health.

Before leaving the subject of sub-human forces, it should be recalled that violent animal forces dominate only in a small minority. Most people have very short periods of violent reaction to the latihan - but there are many who pass through a prolonged stage of apathy, despondence, hesitancy or fear. For these, it is very hard to continue and those who have been able to do so are to be admired, for they act as if they had faith without the consolation of the direct experience. When the hard stage is passed, people previously dominated by negative forces are completely transformed and are a marvel to their friends.

5. The Natural Body

Each stage of development reproduces in itself the seven stages of cosmic completion. Thus, although in the first stage it is only the first or natural body that is transformed, the process is experienced also in all other parts of man. The pure, natural body of man does not respond to negative impulses. The vivification of the limbs and organs of the body makes them sensitive to the quality of the impulses that act upon them.

The sense of relaxation and physical awareness already described is followed by the observation that small, but undesirable, bodily habits lose their hold and disappear by themselves. These are connected with the material forces, and both time and the exercise of patience are required before the body is liberated from all the satanic forces that oppress it. Moreover, it must not be forgotten that nothing in the latihan happens against our own will. Once Pak Subuh was asked how it was that certain bad habits persisted in someone who had followed the latihan for a long time. He smiled and said, "Because he himself does not wish to be free from them. He wishes for spiritual development, but he does not want to change. Later he will see for himself, and then he will begin to wish to change."

The second stage is connected with food and breath. Those with irregularities of breathing - such as asthmatics - begin to observe alleviation of their symptoms. Trainees find that they eat more in accordance with their needs and less according to their appetite. Those accustomed to alcoholic drinks find that their need and desire for alcohol steadily diminishes. At the same time, trainees become more sensitive to the quality of food. They eat less, but it matters more to them whether the food is well prepared or not. In this connection, Pak Subuh has laid emphasis on the great responsibility that attaches to the preparation of food. "Rightly speaking, the cook should be himself or herself in a state of purity - then the food also will be pure, and people will be made happy by eating it."

There is a further stage in which the eyes really begin to see and the ears to hear, when the hands really touch the instruments they use. This quickening of the senses is something unmistakable which scores of people have observed without being told to expect it. At first, the experience is transient, but slowly the new 'natural body' enters into the old body and the sense of 'seeing with one's own eyes' becomes an established fact.

When the organs and limbs are filled with the new life, they begin to obey the voice of conscience, and not that of our own self-will. Thus trainees begin to notice that when unpleasant or malicious thoughts arise in their minds, to which they would habitually give expression, the words stop in their throats and the expression of their face changes by itself. It is chiefly due to this, that friends remark upon the transformation in the appearance of those who follow the latihan.

6. Elimination

The positive results described in the last section are by no means the most obvious consequences of the latihan. There are also negative manifestations, due to the elimination of impurities, or as it is sometimes called, 'throwing out'. The physical organism of man is like a sponge that absorbs all kinds of influences from the moment of birth. Unless he is able to come under the law of 'working from within', the traces of all these influences accumulate in him, and enter his 'personality'.

There are, undoubtedly, some very fine sensitive substances that absorb and store up all these influences, and are responsible, among other things, for the phenomenon of *memory*, that strange and important property of the great life force. I have called them elsewhere the 'sensitive energies'. These energies thus become tainted with all the bad habits of movement, instinct, feeling and thought that are formed in the personality. In the latihan, the far higher energy that is released from the higher centres seeks to fill the organism with new life. It is obstructed by the tainted sensitive energy, which it drives to the surface. The result is that memories lost in the sub-consciousness and habits that are suppressed in external behaviour all begin to produce visible reactions. Put simply, the trainees begin *(a)* to see themselves as they really are, and *(b)* to show themselves to others also in their true character.

This produces, in the early stages of the latihan, situations that can be difficult or embarrassing. It has been observed that in every centre where Subud has started, there has been a period when every kind of personal misunderstanding has run riot. People have quarreled, and disagreed on all kinds of practical issues that ordinarily would be settled without trouble. Doubts, suspicions, jealousy, impatience, wounded vanity - in fact the whole gamut of unpleasant and negative emotions are brought to the surface. Among people accustomed to self-observation, such consequences cause neither surprise nor consternation. Indeed, they are a clear proof that the action of the latihan is a genuine purification.

There is no doubt that the elimination is not merely a change of state, but the effective removal of 'psychic toxins'. The elimination is experienced by the trainee himself as producing a state of inner cleanness. Trainees remark upon the sense of being inwardly clean that they enjoy after the latihan. But while

127

the poison goes out of the trainee, it can enter into another person whose purification is further advanced, and is therefore more sensitive.

This can result in very unpleasant experiences for the helpers, who are sometimes even physically sick as a result of some uncleanness that has been eliminated by another. Another strange, but unquestionably objective, proof that an actual substance is eliminated is the foetid odour that is often observed in the vicinity of a trainee who is eliminating some unpleasant habit. The odour is perceived by all the helpers present, and it suddenly disappears when the elimination has occurred.

The absorption by one person of the poisons eliminated by another has results that, at first, were very disconcerting. We found that we experienced various negative states without being able to trace their origin. Later it was explained to us by the Indonesian helpers that we were picking these up from other people, and that we could easily get rid of the poison if we were to do a latihan by ourselves or with the other helpers.

For me personally, this threw light upon a problem that had vexed me for many years. I had observed that when I was sitting in front of a group of students following Gurdjieff's exercises, I frequently found myself with a headache, or very exhausted and sometimes physically sick. I had asked other people who were instructing groups, and found that they had the same experience, but ascribed it to their own weakness, being confident that when they could be more fully conscious and stronger in themselves they would cease to be affected. However, as far as I was concerned, this trouble, instead of improving, grew steadily worse, until I really came to dread the days when I had to instruct groups or give general talks.

Very soon after coming to the latihan, I understood for myself exactly what had been happening, and found the way to cleanse myself of the poisons that I had been absorbing. This was for me a real blessing, for I have since been obliged constantly to be with people in whom some kind of elimination was occurring, and have never suffered in the way I did before. Trainees who in the course of their work have to meet sick, mentally disturbed, nervous, angry or simply negative people, have reported the immense benefit it has been to them to be able to 'clean themselves out' by a latihan at the end of such meetings.

All the experiences described in this chapter refer to the first stage of purification, by which the natural body of man is brought to life and filled with the Great Life Force. This is what I understand by the resurrection of the body, for it means that within the mortal perishable body is formed a second body that does not perish when the physical body dies.

8. THE COMPLETION OF MAN

I. *The Sacred Impulses*

THE true man in us is not of this earth and, although he lies sleeping in the depths of our essence, he has not lost the thread that connects him with his Source. From this connection, there arise in us impulses that are truly sacred inasmuch as they are the means whereby we are drawn back towards our place of origin.

Four of the Sacred Impulses are of especial significance for Subud. These are: surrender, patience, trust and sincerity. They do not originate in the mind and the will of man, but they are operative in us only by our own consent. Their connection with the latihan has already been mentioned and by understanding them better we can come to appreciate the true role of human freedom in the completion of our nature.

By *Surrender* is meant not a state of passivity or irresponsibility, but the recognition that we men are not the masters of causes - that is, we cannot 'do'. To see for ourselves that our 'doing' cannot go beyond the mechanical processes of this world and to realize that we must put aside the idea that we can set ourselves free by our own efforts-these are the conditions of surrender. In its full significance, surrender is to place oneself wholly in the hands of God - but we cannot have any idea of what this means until after we have become conscious of the link between our own spirit and the Holy Spirit. In practice, therefore, surrender means to put aside our own desire to 'do' something and to allow the action of the latihan to proceed in us. This has already been explained in connection with 'not-thinking'. Many trainees object when they are told to 'surrender' that they cannot picture to themselves how it is possible to submit oneself to a Power of which one is not even aware. What cannot be pictured or thought about is not necessarily hard to realize in practice. All that is required is that one should consciously and willingly allow all one's functions to work spontaneously and automatically. This 'allowing' is the beginning of surrender.

Patience is the acceptance of the times and seasons that are not of man but of God. So long as we look for or expect results, we hinder the inner working. Impatience is always a manifestation of self-will. Even if our aim is our own perfecting or the true welfare of others, we trip over ourselves if we 'try to go faster than God'. I have referred to the two streams of life and mechanicalness; true patience enables us to be carried safely and surely in the stream of life. All impatience throws us back into the stream of mechanicalness that leads to destruction.

Patience is a sacred impulse. As St. Paul declared, it is one of the manifestations of charity. But true patience can come only from within. Patience imposed from without is weakness.

Trust in God is both the condition and the fruit of spiritual awakening. Trust, like patience, must come from within. Trust of the personality is stupidity. The personality of man cannot trust God and indeed has no reason to do so, for the personality is merely an earthly artefact, not a creature of God.

Trust in God is the assurance that His will is accomplished in all things. Trust in man is the expectation of outward actions, but trust in God is the work of conscience. A pupil asked Ibrahim Khawwas about trust (tawakkul); the story goes on: "He replied 'I have no answer to this question just now, because whatever I say is a mere expression, and it behoves me to answer by my actions; but I am setting out for Mecca: do thou accompany me that thou mayest be answered'. I consented. As we journeyed through the desert, one day an old man rode up to us and dismounted and conversed with Ibrahim for a while; then he left us. I asked Ibrahim to tell me who he was. He replied, 'This is the answer to thy question'.

'How so?' I asked. He said: 'This was the Apostle Khidr, who begged me to let him accompany me, but I refused, for I feared that in his company I might put confidence in him instead of in God, and then my trust in God (*tawakkul*) would have been vitiated'."

Within the working of the laws of nature, there is the manifestation of God's Will directed towards the salvation of creatures: to trust is to rely upon that manifestation without expecting the laws of nature to be violated.

Sincerity means harmony between the inner and outer life. Concerning sincerity, I will quote a passage from the *Kaskf el Mahjoub* of Al Hujwiri.

"Men in their dealings with God fall into two classes. Some imagine that they work for God's sake when they are really working for themselves; and though their work is not done with any worldly motive, they desire a recompense in the next world. Others take ·no thought of reward or punishment in the next world, any more than of ostentation and reputation in this world, but act solely from reverence for the commandments of God. Their love of God requires them to forget every selfish interest while they do His bidding. The former class fancy that what they do for the sake of the next world they do for God's sake, and fail to recognize that the devout have a greater self-interest in devotion than the wicked have in sin, because the sinner's pleasure lasts only for a moment, whereas devotion is a delight forever. Besides, what gain accrues to God from the religious exercises of mankind, or what loss from their non-performance? If all the world acted with the veracity of Abu Bakr, the gain would be wholly theirs, and if with the falsehood of Pharaoh, the loss would be wholly theirs, as God hath said: 'If ye do good, it is to yourselves, and if ye do evil, it is to yourselves.' " (Qur'an xvii, 7.)

Sincerity in the latihan means to be observant and conscious of the reality of one's actions, so as to be aware whether they arise spontaneously from within or whether they are tainted by imagination or imitation. But true sincerity belongs to the whole of life: it is the impulse to be the same outwardly as one is inwardly and the same inwardly as one is outwardly.

Surrender, patience, trust and sincerity are all manifestations of the Conscience that is latent in the depths of the

132

human soul. They are sacred impulses like charity and good will towards men and faith and hope in God. These impulses cannot be simulated by the mind and feelings of man, but must arise spontaneously from within. They work in us only by our consent, but they cannot work unless they are awakened.

Through these sacred impulses man is drawn towards his source and to the place that has been prepared for him beyond all private worlds. They are the means given to us for attaining to complete Manhood.

2. The Seven Stages of Completion

The Subud Emblem symbolizes the seven levels and seven qualities of every completed whole. The ultimate perfection of every created essence requires that it should return to its Source enriched and transformed by having passed through all levels of existence and realized all its possibilities.

Since man is a being incarnated on earth, his completion begins with his earthly body. The first power is that of the material soul. This is subject to the mechanical laws of earthly existence. In Gurdjieff's cosmo-psychology the material soul is represented by the lower or mechanical part of the centres of instinct, movement, feeling and thought. The material soul is earth-bound and can exist only in conjunction with an earthly body of which it is the life-principle.

The second power is not, in the ordinary sense, material, or rather it is composed of substances much finer than those of the physical organism. It is the seat of the strength of the essence. When this soul power is dominated by earthly qualities, its strength is no more than the force of desire. It is polar or dual in nature. For example, it is subject to likes and dislikes, desires and aversions, hopes and fears, and all the other 'pairs of opposites'. When in this state, the vegetative power is not a true soul, but merely the instrument by which a man is attracted to the external world while at the same time enslaved by his own egoism. When the vegetative power is liberated from its identification with earthly attractions, it becomes the main source of strength by which man gains mastery over his physical body.

The third power is that of the animal essence. When dominated by earthly forces - that is the state of unregenerate man - the third soul power is the source of self-will and all motives that flow from self-will. When it is purified it gives unity and consciousness by which a man becomes a stable, independent being.

The fourth is the true human power. Its principle seat is in the sex function. It is the natural human soul that is characteristic of man. When the Human Soul is purified of earthly attachments, it becomes the centre and source of the individuality, of the 'I' that is truly human. There are thus two different conditions of the human soul. The first is that of the man who has become conscious of his real human nature and in whom all the functions are harmonized. The second is that of the man who has achieved individuality and has a permanent self or 'I'.

The fifth degree is that of the complete human being. This cannot be attained by evolution from below. It is a gift of Grace that God bestows upon those human essences chosen to serve His Purposes on the earth. Pak Subuh has said that during the corning Epoch there is the possibility that seventy thousand men of the fifth degree will appear on the earth. If this possibility is fulfilled, human existence on earth will be protected from all disasters that human folly might otherwise bring down upon the race.

The sixth degree is that of the man into whom the Power of Compassion has entered. He is complete within the limits of all finite worlds. It is said that if two hundred such men were present on the earth, all human life would be transformed and there would be peace everywhere. Nothing can be written of the man of the sixth degree, for his highest soul power comes from beyond the knowable worlds.

The seventh and final degree is the soul of the perfect man whose will is eternally conjoined to the Divine Will. No ordinary man can have any conception of this gradation, for the Divine Soul comes from the Source of Creation and is not subject to development or transformation.

If we accomplish the journey of self-completion, we have to pass through the various stages of training and purification. A fourfold preparation is needed before the real man - the Man of the Soul - can find a home in our essence. The fourth degree is a meeting point of the two streams of evolution and involution. By the first stream, man rises from the material world to acquire his own human soul, by the second stream the Holy Spirit descends upon man to endow him with an immortal spirit. When the two are joined and become one soul and one spirit, then comes forth the complete man of the fifth degree. No man can, by his own merit, pass beyond the fourth degree. The immortal spirit of the complete man is bestowed by the Grace of God.

3. Gradations and Stages

In the last chapter I described some of the observations made at Coombe Springs by trainees who have entered the first stage of purification. I did not attempt to assign any particular order or sequence to these experiences - simply because I do not understand them well enough.

I shall set down some of the explanations that Pak Subuh himself has given. This is contrary to his own dictum, "Experience first; explanation second", which reminds me of my old friend Clarence Seyler's advice to young scientists, "Facts first, and then more facts, and theories after". Even this safeguard does not wholly suffice, for it is not easy to distinguish spiritual realities from subjective imaginings. However, even this hazard can be surmounted by patience and persistence - one great merit of the latihan is that in it we come to see ourselves only too clearly and to know when it is our own voice that imitates the tongues of angels.

The first act in the drama of purification is enacted upon the level of our earthly existence. If experiences belonging to a higher world come, they do so only as fleeting glimpses that we must learn to assess at their true value. They are signs of things to come, not evidences of attainment.

In the material world are reproduced each of the seven conditions of the soul. For example, Pak Subuh speaks of saints and prophets of the material world. Solomon represents the archetype of the prophet of materiality: he had great powers, but all came from the material forces. Pak Subuh called him once "the prophet of the successful man of affairs!" Those who are satisfied with earthly existence can, through the latihan, pass through all the seven gradations and acquire health, wealth and power, but remain attached to the earth and must return to it again and again.

The second stage is beyond sense experience. It belongs to the world of the Vegetable Essences. This world is the first of the Abodes of the Blessed. Three transitional stages lead from our earthly existence to this Abode. Each of these three spheres corresponds to a particular condition of spiritual purity, when a man ceases to be affected by material forces. Only when the human power is liberated from the material forces can the soul enter these heavenly realms.

The energies of the First Abode are much finer than those of the world of material objects and they can be perceived by man only when his senses are purified. Although a man may have the qualities that correspond to this world, he cannot enter it until he is prepared. Thus there can be men whose soul qualities correspond to the second and third degrees who are nevertheless wholly dominated by material forces and therefore can know only earthly existence. We have therefore to distinguish again between *levels* and *qualities*. Failure to make this distinction can lead to mistakes regarding the stage which a given person appears to have reached. The Sufis distinguish between *hal* or state and *makam* or station. In conversations with Arab and Turkish Sufis, I have tried to get explanations of these two words, but was never fully satisfied that they were understood. One of the remarkable features of the latihan is the light thrown upon the obscurities of various systems and

136

teachings. It has undoubtedly helped me, more than anything I have met, to understand Gurdjieff's cosmo-psychology, but it is equally illuminating in the new meaning it brings to all mystical literature. It is by an accident of birth that Pak Subuh has chosen the Sufi terminology to describe the stages of the Subud path. Systems are like maps - they are amusement for the man who stays at home and dreams of travel, but a very real help to the man who journeys through unknown country.

I make these comments here because it was only through the latihan that I came to realize the all-important distinction between a quality or *hal* that can be experienced and a level or gradation or *makam* that can be one's home or Abode. Many people are deceived by 'experiences' and imagine that they are evidence of attainment of a higher level of being. The *makam* or station can be occupied only if one has the necessary powers - that is the organs, limbs, modes of perceptions and a body of the requisite fineness of substance to be able to exist upon the level in question.

This is illustrated by the transition region between the first and second worlds. This region contains three stations or 'heavens'. These are often described in mystical literature. When I have read about them I have passed them over as incomprehensible. In the latihan, the reality of these interme-diate stations is unquestionable. More than one trainee has 'seen' the first heaven as a vast expanse of blue ocean, and has realized that it could not be entered with one's ordinary body. The value of such experiences is enhanced by the fact that they occurred to people who had never heard of these Abodes and their significance.

The possibility of entering the intermediate stations or heavens while still on this earth depends upon purification.

4. Human Responsibility

Many of us have been shocked by Descartes' supposed indifference to animal suffering, but if we read his own words, we can see that he is really concerned with responsibility.

Responsibility is an attribute of the soul. It can be put more strongly: an irresponsible soul is not a soul at all. Machines, plants and animals are not responsible, but man is responsible. Hence it follows that man alone of the four categories of existence has a soul.

This would be sound enough reasoning if men were, in fact, responsible and if we were quite clear that the word 'responsible' has the same meaning as applied to different kinds of beings. A young child is a human being and yet not responsible, but it does not follow that it has no soul; but only that the soul is asleep, or inarticulate, or unable to exercise its powers until the child has become a man or a woman. There cannot be responsibility without the power of choice, without the perceptions and knowledge and experience necessary for making a choice.

It seems, then, that responsibility is not a fixed, unvarying property of the soul. Until it is developed the child is inevitably· dependent on others. There is still responsibility, but it is directed towards the helpless child until such time as the direction can be reversed and responsibility can flow outwards.

Responsibility occupies a very important - indeed a central - place in Subud: for the point of responsibility is the centre of the human soul. Only it must be understood that the outer man, the trained, educated personality, can have only an artificial, even a fictitious, responsibility. It is artificial because it comes from outside and not from within. It is fictitious because it implies the exercise of powers which the personality does not possess. Descartes was right in his conviction that true responsibility on earth resides in the human soul but; utterly wrong in assuming that the human soul is awake and active in all men and women.

All experience teaches us that true responsibility only enters a man when his soul is awakened and the subordinate instruments recognize its authority. There is, however, in Subud a more precise lesson to be learned. This concerns the limits of our true, effectual responsibility. These can be very simply defined: *a soul is responsible for all that is on a lower level of being than itself: it is not responsible for what is higher.* Thus we are not responsible for the Spirit of God that works in us. We cannot even cooperate with it, except by being what we are: as a plant cooperates with the gardener by being itself and not by trying to understand or do the gardener's work.

In the latihan, we are not responsible, for we deliver ourselves freely into the hands of a Higher Power that is the Source of our existence and can therefore surely be trusted even with our lives. We have no duty to 'learn about' the Spirit, nor to seek for It, nor even to try to cooperate with It or help It in its work. Therefore we are advised not to 'think', not to 'speculate', not to attempt to 'do' anything to hasten or help the process of our inner growth.

But as soon as we turn from the latihan - the worship of God - to our own outer or inner life, we become responsible; for we are in front of levels of existence lower than our own. My human soul is responsible in front of my vegetative reactions or my animal passions because it is a higher form of being than they. I am responsible for all the material objects, all plants, all animals - for they are less conscious and less understanding than myself. HI stand before a human being who is under the domination of material or vegetative or animal forces, I am still responsible, though in a different way.

But most important of all is my responsibility towards myself. As soon as the action of the latihan has awakened in me the power to separate from my own lower forces, I am answerable for the way I use or fail to use this power.

The phrase 'work on oneself' is often used by people with no understanding of what it implies. No one can work on himself unless he is able to separate from himself. A hammer cannot strike the iron until it has been raised above the iron. The potter could not fashion the clay if he were not different from the clay and possessed of a power that the clay does not have. Therefore the first condition of working upon anything is to separate the active agent and the passive material.

139

The Power of the Spirit acts as the third or Reconciling force to remove the conflict between the active and passive sides of our nature, and enables them to exist separately. It also awakens the inner consciousness that makes the passive, or sub-human, elements visible, 'outside' our real selves. When we are in this state we really can 'work on ourselves' and then we are responsible for our own state and our own conduct. Evidently, the more conscious a human being becomes, the more that man or woman is responsible.

The first responsibility is for our own external manifestations. When we can see for ourselves what is right conduct and we know that it is in our power to do what we see to be right - we are obliged to make the necessary effort. This may mean a struggle with habits, inclinations and with our automatic reactions. If we evade this struggle, we deny the Spirit that has made it possible for us to see.

Later., the separation of affirming and denying forces goes deeper and we become able to separate, not only from our manifestations and so regulate our conduct, but from our reactions. This is the beginning of real freedom, for it means that our likes and dislikes, hopes and fears, pleasures and pains all cease to be 'inside' us and are observed and seen as the working of sub-human or vegetative forces. When we are able to be free from likes and dislikes, a new responsibility enters; for we have then the obligation of being impartial in all our dealings with situations and people.

This brief sketch should be sufficient to show that although in the latihan and in our worship of God we can do nothing of ourselves, when it comes to our relationship with the lower forces, whether internal or external, we can and must be responsible. Work on ourselves, struggle with our own lower forces, is not merely a duty, it is an inner necessity if the work of the Spirit is to develop freely in us.

5. The Purification of the Feelings

I shall write about my own experience of the second stage,

without wishing to suggest that I know anything of its completion or of the experience of higher worlds.

The first recognition that something was beginning to change in my feelings came when, for several days, I found myself almost uninterruptedly in a state of self .• observation. Not only could I see myself as I then was, but I could not help doing so. Moreover, I could see my past life as a whole, with all the mistakes I had made, and the harm that I had done to myself and to others. This was an indescribably painful experience, and I had no idea when it would end. At that time Pak Subuh was still in Indonesia, and I was so desperate about my condition that I wrote to him for advice - the first letter that I had ever attempted in the Indonesian language that I had begun to study. His reply was to the effect that this stage was necessary and would soon pass: by the time I had received his letter, the experience - in that form - was over. But I began to live in a state of 'separation' in which I was aware of two distinct lives constantly present in me. This coincided with a great increase in sensitivity, so that I found that I was aware of the bodily and emotional states of people who were near me, or even about whom I happened to be thinking.

I received at this time one of the greatest blessings of my life - that is, to find myself liberated from the exasperating sexual attraction that Gurdjieff calls 'type and polarity'. I write of this personal experience because to me it was clear proof of the purity and rightness of the Force that works in the latihan. For years I had wrestled with this problem, and although I had learned more or less to discipline my external behaviour, I had never found the way to be free from the inward action of this force. The freedom that is received through the latihan is entirely different from the weakening or mortification of the sexual impulses that is achieved by ascetic practices. On the contrary, the natural powers are brought to life and invested with an entirely new quality. The difference is that they acquire an inherent discrimination that automatically stops them from flowing outside their legitimate channels.

141

Pak Subuh insists with unusual firmness upon the sanctity of marriage and upon the terrible harm that results from any kind of sexual promiscuity. I could see for myself that this is not only fundamentally right, but attainable in practice without difficulty or hardship by those who follow the latihan and succeed in entering upon the second stage of purification. It is impossible to describe the sense of gratitude with which one becomes aware that one is free from the action of forces that are so disturbing an influence in human relationships.

The force of sex belongs to the human world; that is, the fourth power of the soul. It is the first of all the human powers, since it enters man at the very moment of conception before his physical body begins to take shape. Although it belongs to the essence, it manifests in all worlds. In the material world, it is simply a force of attraction between men and women and it is without discrimination. In our present age, when people are almost wholly under the influence of material forces, the power of sex has become divorced from its true human significance. It is hard to imagine a much greater blessing for contemporary humanity, than that a means should be given for the purification of the sexual power and the restoration of marriage to the sacred place that it should occupy in the life of man. I am sure, not only from my own experience, but from that of several others, that the latihan does in fact lead to this result.

During the same period, I observed in myself the process of liberation from 'like and dislike'. This is another of the polarities that dominate in the material world. To find oneself drawn to some people and repelled by others is a terrible slavery from which it is hard to free oneself by one's own efforts. However clear to our minds may be the need to be free from personal preferences we can attain this only when we are in a state of inward quiet and detachment. This can be achieved through spiritual exercises, but only for a time. When the effect of the exercise wears off, we return to our usual condition of inward agitation. We get a taste (*hal*) of detachment or non-identification, but we do not reach the Abode (*makam*) where it is a natural state. In

142

the second world, the polar forces of attraction and repulsion are replaced by the triadic relationship of affirming, denying and reconciling impulses. Liberation from like and dislike is far from indifference or apathy. On the contrary, the qualities of situations and of people stand out more vividly than ever before. The difference is that a reconciling force is present that enables one not only to see the positive and negative aspects of every situation, but also to see beyond them to the place they occupy in a larger whole.

This is put rather abstractly. The experience itself cannot be described. It is to feel the duality and conflict in all things, and to see quite dearly that beyond the duality there is a harmony that takes away its sting.

Peace of mind and a cheerful heart are not small blessings. They are the first fruits of the second stage of purification. When Pak Subuh arrived with his Indonesian helpers, we were all impressed by their constant gaiety and the unruffled calm with which they met the chaotic conditions of the first weeks. We could see that these qualities were the outward result of an inner state, or rather of a station, that they had reached and passed. Later we saw that this Abode is one where there is genuine liberation from like and dislike. It is the true non-attachment that is one of the aims of every discipline and system of self-perfecting followed by man.

6. Freedom from Fear

Attachment to the material world is the principal cause of human fears. Men are afraid because they depend upon supports that have no foundation. The personality of man can find safety nowhere. It must therefore constantly suffer, unless it is able to forget its fears. In order to forget, it turns to what seems secure, since it is visible and tangible: that is, to the material world under whose influence it was formed, and to which it really belongs.

Therefore, people are afraid of one another both individually and in the mass - that is 'public opinion'. They depend upon external possessions and are afraid of losing them. They are dimly aware that their personality cannot exist out of this world, and so they fear death.

When the great life force enters the body it drives out fear, but the personality continues for a long time to be the centre of initiative. Consequently, many fears remain until the personality becomes wholly passive. This is attained only in the second stage of purification. If we could see into the heart of man we would find many fears that are deeper than the personality. These come from the realization that even in our essence. we are still blind to reality. We do not know who we are, nor where we are going. Even that part of man - his essence - which is not destroyed by death, is blind, unconscious and helpless. Dying in that state, it is lost and bewildered, and must inevitably be drawn back into some form of earthly existence. To die consciously has always been the aim of people who had any understanding of the real nature of man. But the consciousness that is needed at the moment of death must be of the essence and not of the personality, and unless that consciousness is present, fear of death is inevitable. When I was at school I was made by my headmaster, Lionel Rogers, a true mystic at heart, to learn by heart Robert Bridges' Lines on a Dead Child, which I quote, probably inaccurately, from memory after nearly fifty years:

"Ah, little at best can all our hopes avail us
To ease this sorrow, or cheer us when in the dark
Unwilling, alone, we embark,
And the things we have seen and have known
and have heard of - fail us!"

These lines were somehow a formative factor for my understanding. Two or three years after I had learned them I was severely wounded in France on 21st March, 1918, and I certainly then had the experience of leaving my comatose body and entering into a state of discarnate consciousness. In this condition, I was quite unaware of the presence of other bodies, but I could perceive the inner experiences that were proceeding in people nearby. I then saw without doubt that the fear of death comes from the illusion that our real existence is dependent on our bodies.

Later, when I was slowly recovering and regaining the use of my paralysed left arm, I remembered Bridges' poem, and saw how true it is that the "things we have seen and have known and have heard of fail us", but that we have in us something that is unseen, unknown and unheard of, and that this will never fail us. Only, we need to be conscious of it, if we are to be delivered from fear of the unknown.

I refer to these early experiences of mine because they are directly linked with much that happened to me in the latihan forty years later. I can only describe the state as one of complete clarity as to the continuity of consciousness after death, and the realization that it is the greatest blessing to be able to leave this life and enter into the next - providing one is ready for it. I was able to say, with full assurance of its truth, that my happiest day on this earth would be my last. Constantly to remember one's death, and to know that one is ready for it is, I believe, a characteristic condition of the latihan. With this, comes the end of fear of any of the forces of the material world.

7. Death

No convincing explanation has been given of the wide spread conviction that has persisted since man first appeared on earth, that death is the separation of the soul and the body, except that perhaps it happens to be true. Ancient beliefs as to the manner in which the soul separates from the body have in Europe at least since the Renaissance been thrown aside as worthless superstition. The Christian Church has been in a difficult situation. The early Christians were firm in their belief in the early return of Christ and the resurrection of the body, so that the grave appeared to be no more than a temporary resting place and death a sleep. The centuries passed and the Christian Church has never clearly faced the readjustment that history has imposed on the early belief. The rise of spiritualism in the hundred years since 1850 has been, in part, a response to the deep need of mankind for some guidance in facing the mystery of death. Spiritualism has seemed to many to be a reversion to superstition, but to others it has offered a hope that some positive attitude might be achieved towards death and life beyond its frontier. The doctrine of reincarnation, imported from the East and very little understood, has been seized upon by millions as a plausible explanation of the apparent injustice and incompleteness of life on earth. But neither spiritualism nor reincarnation have proved wholly satisfying. Moreover the evidences for both doctrines once thought to be convincing have proved on closer examination to be elusive and uncertain.

The consequences for human life on earth have been very serious, for they have gone far to destroy the sense of continuity and with it the feeling of responsibility for our actions, that formerly was the chief regulative force in human conduct. Modern man is no less afraid of death than his ancestors, but he no longer takes it seriously for he has no convictions as to what can be done either to prepare for one's own death or to help others before and after they depart from this life. With very few exceptions, dying people are treated by their own families and by the doctors, nurses and others who have care of them as if the physical body alone were important.

The experience of Subud has brought many of us to the conviction that the veil of death is not impenetrable and that it is possible to do very much to help the dying and the dead and thereby immeasurably to enrich life on earth and beautify it.

When the first edition of this book was written, our experience of death in Subud was not sufficient to justify any reference to the subject. I feel able now to set down certain conclusions about which I have no further doubt.

The first is that death is certainly the separation of one part of man from the other. This other consists not only of his bodily organism but all the powers of the organism as such - that is, those which depend upon the flesh and blood, bones and nerves, including sensation and thought. That which separates is the part which can experience the inner sensitive material that has received the imprint of life. This material is not the true soul, but the ghost or spirit in the spiritualist sense and it may or may not contain a human soul. It may have a greater or less degree of organization and permanence.

The second fact which is for me beyond doubt is that death is utterly different according to whether or not a human soul is present in the ghost. This is not the only difference, for death can be terrible or delightful according to the content that has been acquired by the ghost during life. For many years I have been aware of this difference in the presence of a dead body - even if, as at a funeral, I have not seen the corpse. I have been present at a funeral where I was overwhelmed with the realization that the inner content of the dead person had shriveled up like a dried pea and the ghost was completely lost and could have no better fate than ultimately to be dissolved and disappear forever. I have also several times experienced joy and serenity and received the conviction that all was well .with the inner content of the ghost. Far more rarely I have been aware that the ghost itself has dissolved and that a human soul had been set free to go to a higher sphere of existence.

These vague impressions have become far more precise and certain since I have witnessed the death of a number of people who have received the Subud latihan. In all these, I have been aware of the presence of a human soul, though with very different potentialities for further progress.

The third conclusion is that a positive action can occur between the living and the dead. Consequently, the living and the dead can help one another. Since this opens practical possibilities of enormous significance, it is perhaps the most important realization of all. A son can help his dead father to free himself from his own ghost. A mother can help a daughter or a husband a wife and so on. Conversely 'something' from the dead person can be united with the living and endow them with new strength and open fresh possibilities for them.

These strange assertions can only be verified by someone who has passed through the experience for himself.

I can best amplify them by one or two examples.

A Mr. X received a message that his father had died that morning in another country. As soon as possible, one of the Indonesian helpers and I did a latihan with him. My experience was quite unlike that of my usual exercise. I felt myself imprisoned. I fell on the floor doubled up and struggling to be free. Mr. X himself was lying on the ground, now groaning, now sobbing. The Indonesian was chanting, in a deep voice unusual for him, something like a dirge. I felt obliged to struggle to my feet, but had no strength to do so. My anguish was more mental than physical. After a long time I was able to stand and remained with my eyes closed. A great sense of peace came into the room and I saw a tall figure - perhaps eight feet high - standing over the body of Mr. X. It seemed that the figure entered the body and that X himself had been changed. I was aware that the figure was X's father. Soon afterwards the exercise finished.

We were able soon after to speak to Pak Subuh about the experience, and he confirmed that the father's soul had not been ready to continue alone and had entered into X for the completion of his earthly existence. He also predicted that this would result in changes in X's life that subsequently did take place.

A very similar case with a Mr. Y occurred much later, but this time the liberation from the ghost was much easier. On the other hand there was a greater sense of confusion and uncertainty. I ascertained later that Y's father was a clergyman who had lived a good life, but had not understood his own children. Before the latihan I had not known any of this, but became aware that Y's father was confused due to mistaken habits of thought about life and death.

The third example is the experience of my own wife's death through which we passed since this book was first published. This time I was aware that she remained conscious to her last breath. Unexpectedly and to my surprise I found that immediately after she died, I saw the whole of her life as she was seeing it, including events before I had known her and of which I was not previously aware. It was impossible to doubt that she was united with me. For example, I found myself seeing people and understanding them in a manner of which I was incapable and which I had often observed in her.

I could cite perhaps twenty different experiences that have convinced me that a link exists between the living and the dead that is important for both, and that is almost entirely ignored in modern life. Pak Subuh has given us detailed explanations of what can and should happen, but these would go beyond the scope of this book. It is, however, really necessary to emphasize the importance of the process of dying. Here more than anywhere the separation of the physician and the priest is a disaster. The doctor whose attention is wholly directed towards the sick organism can obstruct the task that the priest should perform. The priest, for his part, is usually at a loss in dealing with the situation since he does not rightly understand the process. Recently a priest who came to enquire from me about Subud told me that going to hospital to visit a dying man, the sister in charge of the ward had called him into her room and said "Please, Padre, don't speak about death: it does so upset the patient." Such is the absurd situation into which we have drifted from the failure of physicians and priests, of the State and the Church, to face the reality of the most important event in human life.

8. Further Stages

I am not qualified, from my personal experience, to write about the third and fourth stages. These are the purification of the intellect or understanding, and the purification of the consciousness, that is of the true 'I' or self of man. These stages open the way for man to higher worlds that are far from any ordinary human experience.

Nevertheless, before we reach a certain Abode we are

149

given a taste or glimpse of what it will contain, and I can write of the states that I myself have witnessed.

The first observation concerns language. Several years ago in The Dramatic Universe I wrote about three degrees of authentic language, of which the second belongs to the realm of Being and is symbolical. I said that symbols can convey an unlimited range of meanings, and differ thereby from signs that can have only one meaning. Signs belong to the realms of science and philosophy, whereas symbols belong to the realm of consciousness and being. I added that the third and highest language is that of gesture, which is the direct expression of the will. I do not know how I came to make this distinction, which I certainly did not understand very well at the time.

In the latihan, about the time Pak Subuh arrived in England, I began to see various symbols; some familiar, some quite new to me. Some of these symbols seemed to have a universal meaning - as, for example, when I saw the disc of the sun with the Cross in the midst of it, shining more brightly than the sun itself. Several times I was able to tell Pak Subuh about what I had seen. In nearly every case he showed me that the symbol was an indication of my own state, of my own progress and of my own future, and not a revelation of objective reality. As soon as he gave these explanations I saw that they must be right, and yet I had not seen them for myself.

From this I came to understand in a new way what Gurdjieff had taught about the higher emotional centre. I realized, for example, that the language of this centre is symbolical, and that its power lies in telling us about ourselves, our state and our needs.

I will give only one example of a 'personal' symbol. Once in the latihan I put out my hands and felt that a globe had been placed in them. Its surface was as smooth as glass, and I turned it over and over to make sure it was perfectly spherical. Although my eyes were closed I could see that it was perfectly transparent, like a crystal. It was heavy and yet it had no weight. As I was wondering what it meant, I opened my mouth and this great globe - as large as a pumpkin - entered my mouth and I swallowed it. I could feel it inside myself gradually being absorbed.

All this had no meaning for me whatsoever, but the same evening, after the latihan, I was able to describe it to Pak Subuh. He said that this was to show that my understanding had been purified and that in future I would be able to see the true meaning of ideas presented to me from outside or from within.

Soon after this, I saw a number of symbols that referred to Subud. Once I saw an angel appearing from beyond the sun and bringing a message to the earth, and I understood that this meant that the origin of Subud was from beyond the Solar System. At another time I found myself lifted far above the earth into the space between the earth and the sun. I saw the earth below me as a tiny ball, and then I saw that a great force was taking hold of the earth and shaking it. This I understood to mean that the Power that had sent Subud to the earth was great enough to shake it to its foundations. Whenever such visions have come to me, I have felt myself entirely detached and unmoved by them - almost as if I were being shown pictures in a book that did not concern me personally at all. As soon as the symbols withdrew, the latihan continued as if nothing had happened.

Many times I realized that what was shown to me could not have been expressed in words without being far too definite and committal to be right. Symbolism is not only a powerful language, but also a protection against misunderstanding. A symbol may have many meanings, but we can only apprehend them in so far as we are ready to do so. Verbal communications can be very misleading, for words always seem to have a definite meaning that the mind can grasp. True symbolic language is altogether beyond thought and it must lose the greater part of its content when it is translated into words.

There is, certainly, far more in the further stages of purification than to receive new means of communication. The third stage is essentially that in which our motives are set free from personal elements. For example, there is in man a sacred impulse to *serve*. Often people come to some form of spiritual training for the professed reason that they wish thereby to learn how to do the Will of God and to serve their fellow men. This profession may be quite sincere, within the limitations of the personality that makes it. In the latihan, the trainee begins to see himself as he really is, and he is obliged to acknowledge the impurity of his motives. In the first stages, self-observation affects his feelings and thoughts about himself and perhaps diminishes his self-assurance, but it does not touch the source of his motives - that is, his own self-will. It is not until after the purification of his lower nature that there begins to arise in him a deeper consciousness that enables him to get inside his own motives. This is the only way in which he can be liberated from his self-will and so prepare himself to become a true normal man - that is, one who acts in everything from a full awareness of the reason for his own existence. Then all motives are subordinated to the single motive of achieving manhood and the 'man' becomes a conscious individual, no longer a collection of warring motives hiding a sub-human self-will.

To be a *man* one must become one whole. This may seem simple, but it is far removed from any condition that we know. On this earth, men are not men, but only shadows of shadows. In the latihan, we begin to see our own insubstantiality, and realize that we would not exist at all if we were translated into the world of the true man. In that world, it is necessary to be oneself wholly and without admixture of any sub-human elements. Until this requirement is satisfied we should find ourselves like Peer Gynt standing before the Button Moulder, compelled to admit that there is no one to answer to our name.

9. The Way of Completion

Our life here on earth in the midst of material objects is the lowest to which human consciousness can descend. It does not follow that material objects represent the lowest possible level of existence. On mathematical and physical grounds we can deduce (as is done in *The Dramatic Universe*) that there must also be a null-world in which experience is subjective and illusory. If there can be experience of such a world it must be incapable of distinguishing, even in the material sense, between dreams and reality. Some of us have had experiences in the latihan which prove that it is possible for man to fall into this 'outer darkness' and to realize that if a man descends into that world he loses every semblance of human nature.

The transition from earthly existence to that of the second Abode requires a completely new equipment of organs, faculties, functions and consciousness. Man in his physical body is an earth-bound creature. He has in him the materials from which a second body can grow, but they have neither form nor function. The arising of the second body is an immense trans-formation of the whole nature of man. He is no longer mortal within the limits of earthly existence, but can enter the next life conscious of the way before him. He can see and hear things that our physical eyes and ears cannot perceive. These possibil-ities have been tested and demonstrated to the Subud trainees, who discover that in the latihan they acquire an entirely new sensitivity to impressions that leave no trace upon the senses. All this is connected with what I have called the 'resurrection of the body'. One of the most impressive features of the early stages of Subud is the speed with which trainees begin to be aware of the appearance of a new life within the body, and can verify for themselves that this new life is endowing them with powers that seem almost supernatural. Indeed, in the literal sense, they are supernatural, if we understand by 'nature' this visible world of material objects.

Pak Subuh has many times enabled selected trainees to verify for themselves that existence in the second Abode is entirely different from the world we know; the second body of man is composed of materials so fine that it cannot be injured by material agencies. For example, it cannot be burned by fire. Once, when this was being confirmed by test, I understood how the martyrs who had received the second body were able to enter the fire unmoved, and to pass through death with no disturbance of their inward serenity and without any loss of consciousness.

It is hard to realize that the second body, so often and so lightly spoken of as the 'astral body', is really a completely independent organism that must be equipped with its own organs of perception, its own functions and its own consciousness. Contrary to what is so often asserted in theosophical literature, the second body does not exist in the ordinary man who has not earned it. It must be conceived, developed, born and matured before it can have an independent existence. Without it, the soul that enters the heavenly regions is completely lost, and must inevitably return to the earth and re-enter a body of the first kind.

For man, the way forward is from world to world, until he returns to his Source. In each world, he requires a different body and new instruments to fulfil new functions. Beyond the second body, anything I might write would be mere hearsay. There is no small risk of distorting into nonsense what one has heard but never in any degree experienced. I shall, therefore, not attempt to write about the third and fourth bodies of man, but all teachings that have authentic knowledge agree in affirming that man must acquire four bodies before the soul is ready to receive the divine gifts of the Spirit.

10. The Relationship of the Sexes

The complete human being is achieved through the fusion of the male and female parts of the soul. The myth of Adam represents the undivided state as primary, and the separation of the sexes as subsequent. This is a symbol of generation, for at the moment of conception the parents are united, and the power of sex acts by way of fusion of the male and female gametes. Sexual differentiation is subsequent to the fusion. Thus not only is the force of sex the first to enter the human essence, but it is also that which reunites the separated parts to produce the androgyne fourth gradation of the human essence.

This prepares the place for the entry of the power and attributes of the perfect human soul.

The relationship between the sexes is thus not only the foundation of human existence here on this earth, but also the means whereby the completion of man is realized. This need not imply that the way to completion is closed to the man or the woman who does not wish to marry during their present life here on the earth. All that it does imply is that the unification of the male and female elements of the soul must be accomplished either before or after the death of the physical body.

Here I should refer to some misunderstanding of Pak Subuh's position, owing to his insistence upon the sacred character of marriage and the part it plays in the completion of man. It appeared from this that those who did not marry were in a hopeless situation, and it was even suggested to us, before Pak Subuh's arrival, that unmarried women beyond marriageable age should not be accepted for Subud. In his early talks in England, Pak Subuh gave special attention to married couples, and impressed upon them the mutual need of husband and wife. It was not until later, when we remarked on the very striking progress made by several unmarried men and women, that he gave a further explanation. He said that if the wish to serve God is stronger in a man or a woman than the wish to marry, and if the wish to marry disappears automatically in the latihan, then it is possible for such a person to pass through all the stages of preparation in this life and come to the unification of the soul-that is, to meet with their true spouse - after death.

He added, however, that this is no justification of the monastic life in general. The monastic vocation is exceedingly rare, and it happens too frequently that Christians and Buddhists (the two religions in which monasticism is widespread) enter the solitary life in imitation of the Christ or the Buddha. The two situations are quite different, and Buddhism does not greatly concern us here. Jesus Christ was and is eternally the perfect Man Who possesses the complete sevenfold nature that is in the origin of Creation itself. Jesus,

155

alone among men, was born with the complete soul in which male and female is undivided. He, therefore, alone among men, had no need for marriage in order to fulfil His mission here on earth. He represents, not only for professing Christians, but for all men of all faiths, the ideal of human purity and perfection. But this does not mean that He can be imitated. Indeed, it is blasphemy for man born of woman to suppose that he can imitate the life of the incarnated Son of God. Jesus having come to the world with the complete human soul received also the Divine Soul from God, and so was in a true sense both Son of Man and Son of God. All conditions were, and are eternally, not merely different but infinitely different, for a Man already complete and perfect in both the human and the divine worlds and for one who is upon the way to the completion of his human nature and preparation for the Grace which was already in Christ before He came to the earth.

Therefore those who suppose that the virginity of Christ and His Mother Mary is in any way like human virginity are in grave error. Their virginity was present in them because they were already complete, whereas human virginity is the rejection of completion. The refusal of marriage can only be justified when it is made with the humility of one who is conscious of his inadequacy, not with the arrogance of one who deems that he has chosen the 'better way'. When the inferiority of the unmarried state is fully recognized and accepted, it need not be a bar to progress any more than all the other defects that are present in human nature and human life on earth.

The relationship of the sexes is entirely different in different worlds. In the material world it is a blind attractive force without discrimination. In the vegetable world, it is the polarity of type and essence. In the animal world, it is the transformation and purification of motives. In the human world, it is the unification of the soul. In ordinary human experience, the three higher modes of sexual relatedness are unknown. But by the law of sevenfoldness all seven qualities are repeated on all levels - hence ordinary men and women can experience some of the *qualities* of the fuller relationships, but not possess their *essence*. From this arises all that sadness in the lives of men and women that comes from seeing glimpses of the unattainable. The full glory of the married state is revealed only to those who can reach the fourth stage of human completeness and discover for themselves what is meant by the words: "They shall become one flesh."

The completion of marriage certainly requires the procreation of children. Since nearly all men and women living on the earth are spiritually unborn, they can have children only upon the material level of existence - that is, under the laws of this earth. Ideally, a man should wait to have children until his own soul is awakened. The reason for this is that at the moment of conception, when the essence is in a state of pure receptivity, it is open to every kind of influence. A pure state in the parents is the only protection against the entry of sub-human soul substance. This is not the only reason why parenthood can be right only when rightly timed. We need to be protected against mechanicalness, which we can visualize as a great stream that flows from the past through the present into the future, carrying with it the consequences of all future events. We have no power to arrest this stream or change its course. But the higher parts of the soul are not subject to the laws of cause and effect.

This is why Pak Subuh has said that the latihan is a frontier through which the stream of causality cannot pass. It is literally true that the iniquities of the fathers are visited upon the children unto the third and fourth generation. The terrible scourge of the past threatens the health, happiness, character, and the very possibility of completion of our children and grandchildren. Many a parent can dimly sense the tragedy of the situation but see also that he is powerless to change it. One of the greatest blessings of the latihan is its power to obliterate the past and set us and our children free to enter the future without the burden of sins that they themselves have not committed. The purification of the sexual life belongs pre-eminently to the fourth stage of completion that is, the truly human stage. It is only when they are truly human beings that husband and wife can be joined in the full union that is the reality of marriage. Indeed, it is only to such a marriage that the words "Whom God hath joined, let no man put asunder" truly apply. Such people are blessed in their union, and they are blessed in their children, in whom a human soul can arise even before they reach the age of responsibility.

We cannot leave this subject without making clear the position of those who treat the sexual relationship lightly. In the sexual act there is a contact between the male and female essences, and whether it is made in wedlock or in wanton promiscuity it leaves its mark upon the essence. Since woman is the passive or, more correctly, the receptive element of the complete soul, the results of the contact are stored up in her. She, therefore, inevitably must suffer if the relationship is broken. Men who take advantage of the receptivity of woman commit a grave injustice, for which sooner or later they must atone. That these are no empty words can be seen in the latihan, when men whose sexual lives have been irregular have to pass through a period of purgation before they can be liberated from the results. But in this earthly existence where the material soul is dominant, it is not men but women who chiefly suffer the consequences of broken unions. The mysterious laws of the interpenetration of essences act in such a way that, if a man comes into sexual contact with a woman who has had many irregular relationships, he picks up the influences of the other men, and his own state is thereby poisoned. We were given a vivid picture of a wealthy Japanese whose sexual life had been deplorable, and who when he came to the latihan began to throw out the characteristics of many men he had not even known.

It must, therefore, be understood that it is equally disastrous for men and for women to allow themselves sexual irregularity. Nothing traps us more helplessly in the stream of mechanicalness, or does more to diminish our potentialities, than to allow our essence to become contaminated with the results of other people's lives. This we do when, without discrimination, we come into the essence-contact that is inseparable from the sexual act.

Thus it is rightly said that the power of sex can be the greatest curse of man, and that it can and should be the greatest blessing. By sex our humanity can be degraded and by sex it can be perfected. As long as people are still in the early stages of purification, they must be protected against the power of sex. For the complete man sex has no longer any outward force, for the cleavage of the male and female elements has been healed.

When I started to write this section, in a suburb of Munich, where I have come to be with Pak Subuh, I would have said that to my knowledge no man had opened any woman but his own wife without incurring serious consequences. I had never heard of Pak Subuh himself opening a woman, not because of possible harm to himself, but because she might place her trust in him and not in God.

By one of the countless strange coincidences of Subud, it happened that I had to speak to Pak Subuh about some letters I had received, and while I was with him an old German woman of seventy-eight years came into the house and asked to see him. Although we were all snowed under with work, he went and spoke to her, and learned that she had been for five years a widow, was totally deaf, and could not sleep for terrible noises in her head. She begged him to help her. We wrote on a sheet of paper that Pak Subuh is not a healer, but she sat weeping in her chair, moaning that she must go mad if the pains continued. I could see that she was already afflicted with senile dementia. After testing her condition, Pak Subuh at first advised that she should drink the juice of a tamarind every evening. When he learned that tamarinds are unobtainable in Germany, he told her to close her eyes. Then, without any explanation, he stood before her and opened her, with myself and two other men, who had been trying to interpret for her, standing by. After about fifteen minutes she was opened. When told to open her

159

eyes she said that the pains had gone. An American trainee drove her back to her house, where she was to renew latihan by repeating the Lord's Prayer each evening before going to bed. I should add that a contact had also been made with her dead husband. I also remembered the saying, "Thy faith hath made thee whole".

11. The Three Higher Constituents of the Soul

The complete man, or man of the fifth degree, is not a product of evolution alone. Pak Subuh has repeatedly emphasized that the fifth power is a superhuman soul. It does not belong to the human world, but descends upon man from above, when he is ready and when he is needed. It has already been noted that 70,000 men endowed with the fifth power of the soul could arise in the world in the coming Epoch. Beyond the fifth level is the far higher, truly Sacred Essence of the compassionate soul. Pak Subuh has said that one such soul could save a million others. The seventh and highest spirit comes direct from God: it is the soul that distinguishes the great Prophets from all other beings who have appeared on the earth.

We have thus a complete scheme to represent all stages of evolution possible for the human soul. In its ultimate perfection, the soul is sevenfold. But the lower souls can be taken up and left like clothing. The three higher souls are beyond individuality, and can enter into many human forms at once. The soul of the Saint can enter into thousands of people and bring them into that profound unity of will and consciousness that is the Communion of Saints.

I have already written too much of matters that are beyond my understanding. I have included these hints chiefly to give some meaning to the statement that the way of perfection for man leads on and on without limit.

9. THE POTENTIALITIES
OF SUBUD

I. The Real Miracle of Subud

AMIDST the welter of impressions engendered by Subud and its action upon people, two clearly established facts stand out as supremely significant. One is the reality of the contact, and the other its independence of any particular person - even of Pak Subuh himself. Since I myself did not believe that such an effect was possible, and nothing that I had ever heard or read about suggested that anything similar has occurred before in known human history, I was for some time sceptical as to its reality. When I saw for myself that more than a thousand people were able to receive the contact merely by asking for it, I was obliged to accept that a miracle had happened. By 'miracle' I understand the direct intervention of the Power of the Holy Spirit in human life, in such a manner as to make possible an event that does not violate the laws of nature and yet could not be brought about by any natural agency, including the will of man himself. There is, I believe, another characteristic of miracles that is commonly overlooked - that is, their perfect timeliness. Miracles do not occur either capriciously, without apparent rhyme or reason, nor do they occur just when someone happens to want them or look for them. They occur only when they are necessary for the renewal of human faith. I believe that isolated or sporadic miracles have occurred and still do occur, and that they are always timely and effectual. Mass miracles of the kind attributed to St. Bernard of Clairvaux must surely have been the work of mass suggestion, and should be discounted.

The miracle of Subud is neither isolated nor is it explicable by the power of suggestion acting upon a crowd. It came to me when I was alone and completely sceptical as to the possibility of any essential change in human nature otherwise than by conscious labour and intentional suffering. It required the cumulative evidence of nearly two months' constant practice of the latihan to convince me that a miracle had really occurred. Those who shared the experiment with me during the months before Pak Subuh came to England were men and women who for long years had been trained in impartial self-observation, and were so well aware of the immense difficulty of an authentic inner transformation that they had even become doubtful whether it was possible to follow Gurdjieff's system without his personal help and guidance. We were convinced by the latihan against our own firmly established belief that there is no easy way to develop the potentialities latent in man. This does not mean that we doubted the possibility, or that we did not believe that the possibility itself is given to us by the Will of God. We doubted only that we could hope to find a means that would really work for us such as we were.

Even when we saw for ourselves that Subud worked in us, we were still so presumptuous as to think that it must require preparation, and that only those could receive it who had already gone a long way towards realizing their own nothingness and were ready to ask for help without expecting any easy way out. Once again, we found that the miracle was far greater than we had imagined possible. Within two months of Pak Subuh's arrival more than five hundred men and women had asked for and received the contact. Among them some, with little or no experience of the spiritual search, made progress that was clearer and more rapid than that of others with every apparent advantage of preparation, combined with greater intellectual powers and more energy and determination. All our preconceived plans for the gradual introduction of Subud, starting with a few carefully chosen and serious people, went by the board.

What occurred was an explosion of the very kind that I had learned to expect as the first stage of any great step forward in natural or human evolution. I could see, moreover, that there was no suspension of the natural order. The powers that I could see emerging in so many people were those that I already knew to be latent in the very nature of man. The miracle was that the process should be set in train so surely and so easily just for the asking. Moreover, I soon realized that my early scruples were unfounded. There is in Subud no question of 'something for nothing', nor any violation of the principle that everything worth having must be paid for. One has to sacrifice and to suffer - but it is consciously and intentionally that one does so, because one sees where one is going and what has to be done.[1] There are great burdens to be borne, but one sees the reason for them, and one is given the strength to carry them.

The miracle is thus the *total* one - that a new possibility has been opened for mankind that is beyond our power to understand, and that we could never have discovered for ourselves. Isolated cases could have been explained away. The fulfilment of prophecies and the realization of predictions carry little weight with the sceptical. The instances of healing of disease that we have so far observed have little evidential value. The strange confluence of people from all over the world may be no more than a coincidence. The fact that remains incontestable is that within sixteen months more than three thousand men and women have found a new force working in them, the power and the beneficence of which they cannot doubt. They have seen, moreover, that this force is quite independent of the presence of Pak Subuh himself, and that it works in all people who ask for it and who can find the way to put aside the obstruction of their own thoughts and imaginations.

2. *The Visible Evidence*

In Chapter 7, I have tried to describe some of the inner changes that occur in the trainees. There are also changes in

---

1   In the last part of *All and Everything*, with the title *"Life is Real Only Then, When I Am"*, that Gurdjieff wrote in 1933, he refers to the difference between 'voluntary' and 'intentional' suffering. It is not voluntary self-imposed suffering that is required, but intentional to submit oneself to a process in which suffering is inevitable.

the outer life that can be observed and verified by others. After the first influx of people who had been prepared for Subud by study of Gurdjieff's system, a new flow began of people attracted chiefly by manifest changes for the better in their relations and friends. A group of examples comprising at least two score of people is particularly significant. Among those who had been members of groups following Gurdjieff's system were many whose husbands or wives or parents or children had been hostile to the work, and painful situations had arisen, in which jealousy and a sense of injustice at being deprived of companionship had embittered family relationships. We observed with real surprise that within one or two months of the coming of Subud, these 'recalcitrant' relatives were asking to come to the latihan, because they observed such unmistakable improvements in those who had come.

A second group of examples can be taken from a number of mentally or emotionally unstable men and women who came to Subud, and were admitted with some reluctance and trepidation on the part of all but Pak Subuh himself and his Indonesian helpers. We feared that the stimulus of the latihan might result in over-excitement, in outbreaks of manic conditions or of hysteria. The very opposite occurred. Although the response was by no means always the same, in the majority of cases the latihan calmed the excitable and brought about a marked improvement in sufferers from mild schizophrenia and manic-depressive states.

On the other hand it also happened that some people outwardly normal and apparently stable began in the latihan to show symptoms of some deep-seated disturbance. The effect of the latihan appeared similar to that of· a well-conducted psycho-analysis, without the grave disadvantages of the latter that a large proportion of patients remain dependent upon the analyst. The potentialities of Subud in helping psychopathic conditions are still almost wholly unexplored. I am concerned here only with the impression made upon people who have seen their friends and relations, previously disturbed, made calm and able to meet life with more confidence than ever before.

One interesting suggestion may here be mentioned. This is the possibility of rehabilitating criminals. We have no direct evidence in England, but we have heard of several cases in other countries where criminals, including more than one professional murderer, have come to the latihan and have been completely liberated from the impulses to steal, rob or murder. Since the criminal's problem is usually not absence of desire to change, but the inability to persist in the face of temptation, there is no reason why he should not ask for and receive the latihan and find therefrom the strength that he lacks.

3. Subud and the Family

The degeneration of family life is one of the distressing symptoms of our modern world. The increasing incidence of divorce - one per cent in 1911 to 6·7 per cent in 1954 - is of less importance that the far greater proportion of 'unhappy' marriages which 'somehow or other' are kept going. The isolation of young married couples from the parental hearth leads to the breakdown of the family unit, which should comprise three generations. It is true that many old people are given homes by their married children - but this seldom repairs the family unity which has been broken. Anyone with long experience of helping people with their personal problems, as I have had for nearly thirty years, knows that the tensions of married life are the main cause of all psychological disturbances, whether in the parents themselves or by a delayed action upon the children.

Therefore any means whereby a real help can be brought to a disturbed family should be regarded as a major blessing for mankind. To facilitate the dissolution of marriages that fail is merely to admit a deeper spiritual failure. No evil is cured by alleviating its consequences. Help can come only from within - that is, by the awakening of the soul to the reality of the bond between the sexes.

One of the palpable benefits of the latihan has been in the help it has given to scores of married couples in varying degrees of distress. We have even observed several instances of actual separation where without any external pressure or persuasion a wife has returned to her husband or a husband to his wife. Certainly, so long as the purification is still in the first stage, the difficulties do not disappear. The change of inner attitude has, however, in nearly all cases been sufficiently definite and permanent to enable those difficulties to be faced as they never were faced before by the people concerned.

The benefits of the latihan are equally evident in happy marriages. Even at best there cannot be complete compatibility between two incomplete people. Pak Subuh has said that every woman has seven needs that she looks to her husband to satisfy. These correspond to the seven basic qualities in every human essence. No ordinary husband can satisfy all the seven needs. It is indeed a fortunate couple who can find two points of true mutual completion. In the latihan, latent qualities are developed in the husband so that he and his wife become more fully partners of one another in all that they need. An exclusive mutual attraction between husband and wife takes the place of the undiscriminating sexual impulse. This creates a force that can overcome all difficulties.

When the second stage of purification is reached, the sexual relation itself is completely transformed. It is liberated from passion and desire, and becomes instead the fulfilment of the need for mutual completion.

All these are results that we have actually observed, and they have given us confidence that the progress of Subud can do more than any other factor to restore the sexual relationship to its true position in human life.

Not all married couples are compatible in essence. Where there is real incompatibility there cannot be true marriage. On the whole, such cases are rare, for the potentialities of each essence are exceedingly great, and a given man or a given woman may hope to find a true partner within a very wide range of essences. Incompatibilities of personality are far more frequent than those of essence, but even where a really painful or unpleasant tension exists between two personalities, the purification of the feelings can uncover the essence-possibilities of a successful union. Properly speaking, therefore, divorce should be reserved for cases of proved incompatibility of essences, and not based upon an artificial code of marital behaviour. Adultery and desertion are not sufficient grounds for divorce, nor are their absence any assurance of a true marriage. It will be a long time before these fundamental principles are understood and acted upon. Meanwhile we can look to Subud as a very present help for all married couples. This is important not only for the man and wife, but even more so for their descendants. Subud is a frontier at which the past is arrested, and it can make possible a fresh beginning in almost every kind of human trouble.

4. Subud and Society

Social problems are mainly connected with motives. Difficulties arise because people's motives are not pure, and so they suspect one another. Moreover, through the operation of various kinds of magic, imaginary motives are created. People come to believe that many things are indispensable for their happiness that are not only useless but often causes of the very unhappiness or unrest of which they complain. Fear, suspicion, jealousy, false pride, ambition, greed, indifference to the sufferings of others and the other evil forces in human life, distort all motives and bring about the degeneration of every attempt to create a normal, harmonious human society. The sacred impulses that are really present in all men include kindliness, good will, the desire to serve and to help one another. The two kinds of motives become mixed, and so, when men wish to establish an ideal society they usually end by shooting people - to make a better world. Even when there is no shooting, the promised ideal society turns either into a tyranny of well-meaning busybodies, or into an instrument for depriving men of self-reliance and the capacity for independent initiative and judgment and of the desire to work hard to supply their real needs.

This is not intended as a criticism of the modern world or a denial of human progress. In every past Epoch it has been the same. The same evil forces that destroyed the heroic age - the Hemitheandric Epoch - led the Megalanthropic Epoch into useless wars, revolution and spiritual degeneration. And yet, in many deeply significant ways, mankind in the twentieth century is more enlightened and enjoys a better social order than in former times. Only, as I showed in the introduction, we are seriously threatened by the growing power of the external material forces, and if progress is to be maintained and stabilized, a general spiritual awakening is indispensable. The outer world forces have grown so powerful that fear, suspicion, greed and the rest have a greater potency for destruction than ever before.

The only way out - as indeed is widely recognized by serious people all over the world-is the purification of motives. It need hardly be said that this cannot be achieved by advice, or threats, or good example, or by any kind of organized activity.[1] The only test is whether a proposed means does actually work in practice. When this is applied to Subud, we find most hopeful indications. For more than twelve years we have at Coombe Springs experimented with a loose form of community in which fifty or more people of diverse interests, ages, education, social status and even of different races and creeds have lived and worked together. Thanks to the discipline of self-observation and personal effort, as well as the spiritual exercises we had received from Gurdjieff, we were able to surmount many of the difficulties that arise from 'mixed motives'. But it could not be said that a real harmony was ever achieved. Moreover, as always in such communities that are based on 'working from without', the whole structure was too much dependent upon me personally, as the supposed 'leader' or 'teacher' of the groups.

When Subud came to England, the conflicts and

---

1   Such as public education, youth movements, religious revivals, welfare organizations or societies for the promotion of good will and international brotherhood.

misunderstanding described in Chapter 7 threatened considerable disruption. In the early stages, the latihan, so far from helping, brought the negative forces to the surface and made matters outwardly worse. Within six or seven months, there was an unmistakable transformation. We can see the early beginnings of a future society in which each member accepts and takes responsibility for himself, and at the same time is able to respect the views of other people and work harmoniously with them.

Subud has been with us for only sixteen months, and it is too early to expect results that would be obvious to any casual observer. But to those of us who have watched the whole process over many years, there can be no doubt that Subud is a social force that can work the miracle for which we are all waiting: to make it possible for mankind to make full use of all the marvellous achievements of modern science and technology without destroying everything - including mankind itself - through the scourge of 'mixed motives'. The ideal society cannot be based upon leadership, for this implies dependence of the many upon the few, St. Paul's analogy of the human organism still remaining the truest picture. Only when each member is ready to accept his own place and fill it, can there be an organic society. But so long as motives remain attached to earthly interests, the acceptance of one's place degenerates into slavery. It is hard to represent to oneself how all human relationships could be transformed if the effect that we have seen among a few hundred were to be shared by millions. This is no longer an abstract ideal, but a practical possibility. It will be a society in which guidance will take the place of leadership, in which authority will be looked upon as a burden to be borne rather than an ambition to be attained, and in which the desire to occupy a place for which one is not fitted will give way to the realization that everyone can have what is most precious in human life - contentment and security and the assurance of eternal welfare. In such a society all the outer-world achievements of mankind can be a blessing, and there will be no need to preach, like Gandhi, a return to the 'home-spun' life of the past.

5. Subud and Religion

With all its extraordinary power for good, Subud cannot achieve its object unless it is brought into the established religious life of mankind. Pak Subuh has repeatedly insisted that Subud is not a new religion, and that it offers no new dogma, no new forms of worship, no new church. If Subud had appeared as a movement of renewal within the Church - like the Franciscan Order or the Society of Jesus - it would have presented no special problems. The complete submission to the authority of the Church that characterized a St. Francis or a St. Ignatius would have assured the acceptance of so manifestly sincere a contribution to piety and faith.

Had Pak Subuh himself consented to remain no more than a pious Moslem, he would undoubtedly have been accepted by the Ulema of Java as a man through whom trust in God could have been restored, and religion given a renewed strength among the Moslems of the Malayan Archipelago. It is chiefly, perhaps solely, his catholicism that has so far impeded the acceptance of Subud as a movement of Islamic revival among his own people.

It must be difficult to accept the thesis that there can be a revival of religious faith, the source of which is outside a Church, without fear of disturbance of dogma or authority within the Church. Lay movements of reform, even when held within the framework of established religion, have often proved dangerous, and have led to schisms and heresies. The very notion of a world-wide religious revival suggests eclecticism of the kind that reduces religion to a system of universal morality, and faith to a colourless theism.

It has been amply demonstrated that true religion cannot be restored by any form of propaganda or mass suggestion. The immense and sincere efforts that have been made by the Christian Churches since the end of the war have done little to restore faith. The Islamic revival that is an unmistakable fact for anyone who has travelled in South West Asia has brought fanaticism in place of faith, and has utterly failed to come to terms with the realities of the modern world. I have no first-hand knowledge of the revival of Buddhism in the Far East, but competent observers have told me that little has been accomplished - chiefly owing to the obscurantism of the Buddhist monks, except perhaps in Burma, where the Satipatthana movement has become a real force. Even so, this system of organized meditation is rather a method of 'working from without' than a way to the renewal of religious faith.

All this is the more remarkable in that the need for religion is deeply felt throughout the world. The materialism in which the Megalanthropic Epoch has foundered is now discredited, even among many of the natural scientists who were its chief exponents and prophets. The world is waiting for something, but for the most part has no idea what to expect or what to hope for.

We have therefore to face the question whether Subud can fulfil men's hopes and allay their fears. I think the answer chiefly depends upon whether or not Subud can be accepted by religious leaders as a means bestowed upon mankind for the restoration of true worship of God; a way that can be followed without sacrifice of any of the specific dogmas of any religious community, and without diminution of the authority which the Church must maintain and preserve if it is to fulfil its function.

It seems to me that if Subud is rightly understood, it can be accepted by everyone who believes in God and is ready to put his trust in Him alone. The sacred impulses of sincerity, trust in God, surrender of one's own self-will and patience in waiting for God to fulfil His times and seasons, are the foundation of all religious worship. Whoever enters the Presence of God with these gifts will not be deceived. They are all that is asked for in the latihan.

Only the practical test counts. Those who have followed the latihan confirm that so far from being separated from their own confession, they are brought closer to it, and find a new depth and significance in their religious observances. Not only this, but they find that, where previously they were troubled by doubts and scruples concerning some article of faith, they now see that these doubts and scruples were grounded in human thought, and that they can accept literally the truth of their confession. Thus one man recently told me that he found himself in the latihan repeating the Apostles' Creed and seeing for himself that every word he was uttering was true. This had astonished him, for he had previously rejected the Creed as being incompatible with a rational Christianity.

There is, in every great religion, a vast positive content expressed in the form of dogma or teaching. The mind of man cannot understand the dogma, for it belongs to the higher regions of the soul that are inaccessible to thought. Therefore, people either believe or refuse to believe, in both cases without understanding what it is that they accept or reject. When the soul is awakened, it begins to see what the mind cannot think about, and then it knows that what the mind could not grasp is true and necessary for salvation. Tertullian's saying, *Credible est, quia ineptum est, et certum est, quia impossible* ceases to be a paradox for those who follow the latihan.

The positive content of religious dogma is never lost in the latihan. There is, however, a negative content that consists in denying and rejecting the truth of other faiths. This is not religion, but fanaticism or narrow-mindedness. This disappears with the latihan as the trainee sees that all positive religious beliefs are compatible, and that all apparent contradictions spring not from the soul but from the mind, if not indeed from the lower nature of man. So long as the denial and rejection of heresy are thought to be essential to true religious faith, there is certainly a stumbling block.

It is a sign of the times and foretaste of what is prepared for man in the next Epoch - if he will accept it - that religious intolerance is much less prevalent today than in former times. People do not wish to go by the way of denial and rejection, and it is a great merit in the priesthood that they recognize that intolerance has grown much weaker during the present century. Men of all religions are now more ready to accept that Revelations of the Divine Purpose must have reached others who may be outside the community to which they happen to belong.

I myself have no doubt that it is literally true - as Pak Subuh says - that through Subud a Christian will become a better, more conscious, Christian with his faith more firmly grounded than ever before. The deadly enemy of mankind is materialism, which really means belief in this visible world and rejection of other worlds and other possibilities. Materialism is an invidious, satanic enemy, and the mind of man cannot follow all its manoeuvres. Subud is a most powerful weapon against materialism, for it enables people to see beyond it. No earthly weapon can avail, because the material forces do in fact dominate the earthly life, and those who see with earthly eyes only are fully justified in asserting that they can find no evidence of a world that is beyond matter. Materialism cannot be combated with its own weapons, nor upon its own terrain. Like earth-born Antaeus, it thrives and is invincible so long as it can keep its feet upon this earth. When it is lifted above the earth, it weakens and finally succumbs.

The way of deliverance from materialism is the first contribution that Subud has to make to the restoration of faith. The second is the direct conviction that comes to those who follow the latihan that the religious experience is real. This conviction is very rare in the modern world, and even among those who are called to the priesthood it is seldom stable and permanent. This is the cause of acute anguish to many, and in fact several ordained priests have come to Subud in the despairing hope of rediscovering their lost faith, and have not gone away disappointed. The third gift of Subud is trust in God. When this comes to man, his life is transformed. It is even rarer than faith in the reality of religious experience, for many who have the latter continue to suffer from anxiety and doubt as to

173

the fulfilment of Divine Purpose. When there is trust in God, religion is restored to its rightful place as the supreme human concern.

Since these great gifts - liberation from materialism, conviction of the reality of religious experience and trust in God - can be received without sacrificing one jot or tittle of the dogmas of one's own faith, it seems to me that the leaders of religion throughout the world must eventually welcome Subud as the answer to the universal prayer, "O God, make speed to save us!"

I am not foolish enough to suppose that my writings will carry conviction to those who have not experienced Subud, nor do I expect that the acceptance of Subud by the Churches will come quickly. But I believe that it may come, because I am sure that this is the Will of God.

6. The Expansive Power of Subud

We come now to the kernel of the matter: that which distinguishes Subud from any other spiritual gift that has previously been known on the earth. This is the power of expansion that comes from the mode of transmission of the contact. Subud is the manifestation of one of the grand laws of nature that has hitherto been known only in physics and biology. This is now familiar even to laymen as the Law of Chain Reaction, or self-accelerating explosion. It is simply illustrated by the growth of the rabbit population of Australia, or the spread of bracken in Britain. In both cases, a few individuals were imported into a new country where the conditions of existence - soil and nutrients - were wholly favourable. There were few carnivorous animals to keep down the rabbits, and as each mother rabbit can have several litters of half a dozen or more in a year, a pair of rabbits could produce, say, a thousand million descendants in ten years. This happens because each pair born can be the start of a new chain. Even with immense wastage, the rate of growth is prodigious, and, as everyone knows, the whole agriculture of Australia was threatened by the chain-reacting rabbits. Similarly bracken, unknown in England in the eighteenth century, now covers more than half of the common land of the country.

Another example is the chain reaction in nuclear physics that now holds the entire population of the world in suspense. The discovery barely twenty years ago that certain heavy atoms would explode when bombarded with neutrons, and in doing so produced more neutrons that could explode other atoms, has changed the course of human history. The devastating power of the nuclear chain reaction comes from the speed with which the chain renews itself, each generation occupying less than a ten thousand millionth of a second.

If we compare nuclear fission with the conventional explosion, we can see that the latter follows a different law. There is also an exceedingly rapid reaction, but not self-acceleration. The explosion wave is propagated from a centre, and as it moves outwards, its energy is dispersed over a wider and wider radius, and its intensity is correspondingly diminished. All such processes follow what is called the Inverse Square Law. This governs all actions that expand outwards from a centre. It is well known in physics. A less exact form of the law governs the spread of new characters in a biological genus. There is yet another law that operates when the expansive process actually produces factors that resist its own development. This is called in economics the Law of Diminishing Returns, or the principle of saturation.

These laws can be found working - though not in an exact numerical form - also in the spread of ideas and spiritual forces. Let us take the case of a reformer with an immense influence upon his immediate followers. Communicating his zeal to them, he initiates an explosion that soon passes beyond the limits of personal contact with the reformer himself. At second hand, his preaching has less power, and it is transmitted less exactly. The intensity diminishes with distance from the source. Moreover, compromises and misunderstandings are inevitable, and the version of his message that reaches distant places is very unlike the original. Still greater is the diminution and distortion that occur as the message passes through time from generation to generation. Only an initial impulse of immense power can spread, by expansion, through many countries and peoples. The loss of intensity and ultimate loss of content are both inherent in the method of transmission from one man to other men. The source is limited and the channels are obstructed, the flow is uncertain, and finally it comes to a stop.

All movements of spiritual regeneration within the last five thousand years have developed according to these two laws, and the utmost that might be hoped for is that a fresh impulse might come, strong enough to spread widely and affect a sufficiently large number of people to produce a new force in the world.

With Subud, none of these limitations apply. Not being transmitted from person to person by an outward means of communication, but by direct contact with the Source, it does not suffer diminution or distortion. Since the contact can be given many times over by everyone in whom it is fully established, it does not depend upon proximity to the centre from which it originates. It may by now have occurred to the reader that Subud could be described as a 'spiritual chain reaction', and this would be an accurate observation.

The power of expansion of Subud is unlimited because it is not transmitted through a limited channel - that is, through a human being. It can, given suitable conditions, develop at an ever accelerated pace. For example, in England after three months, fourteen people, seven men and seven women, had been authorized to give the contact. One of these, Bulbul Arnold, gave it in Ceylon to one hundred and four women in three weeks.

Gurdjieff's Ashiata Shiemash required that each all-the-rights-possessing brother of his brotherhood should be able to open the conscience of a hundred others, and each of these in turn should be able to open a hundred more. I remember, when

I first read this chapter, making the calculation that even if only four in each hundred acquired the power of transmission and each required one year to transmit it to a hundred others, the whole of mankind could receive it within eighteen years. I was naturally deeply interested when Pak Subuh told us that, if mankind would receive it, Subud could reach the whole world within eighteen years, and that it had been revealed to him that his missionary journeys would continue for the same length of time.

The essence of the chain reaction is that the whole force is transmitted without change or diminution at each step. The tenth generation of rabbits has the same fecundity as the first. The ten thousand millionth atom to undergo nuclear fission produces the same excess of neutrons as the first. When this happens, distance from the point of origin no longer has any importance. Each point of contact becomes a new centre of expansion with exactly the same power as the first.

If Subud has the property, as we believe, of giving a direct contact with the Great Life Force by which all existence is sustained, then it can develop without limit and without diminution, and it can do so very rapidly. The only limit to the expansion of a chain reaction is the exhaustion of suitable 'fissionable' material within reach of the reaction. With Subud this could include the majority of all people living on the earth.

In such an idea there is a vast satisfaction. We are reminded of Milton's description of the war between the powers of light and darkness, in which each of the satanic weapons was matched by an equal, but purer, angelic power. There is a strange fitness in the possibility that the perils into which the material chain reaction has plunged mankind should be averted by another chain reaction - but this time in the spiritual and inner life of man.

7. The Ordinary Man

Subud does not make its appeal to the intellectuals or to those who are in search of some esoteric teaching. It could well be called the 'Path of the Ordinary Man'. It makes no demand beyond what is expressed in the phrase 'ask and it shall be given you'. Such asking does not presuppose any special preparation nor even any special qualities. The scientist or philosopher has no advantage over the mechanic or the bus conductor, but it is also true that he is at no disadvantage. When we look at those who come to the latihan we echo the words "Of a truth, I perceive that God is no respecter of persons". Sometimes we are tempted to go further and say "I thank Thee O Father, Lord of heaven and earth, because Thou hast hid these things from the wise and prudent and hast revealed them unto babes".

The future of the world depends upon the ordinary man. He alone can change the course of history; not the great thinkers nor the powerful rulers of the world. These have had their day. The ordinary man is helpless so long as he remains subject to the power of mass suggestion and depends upon external supports in all that he does in life. But throughout the world, the ordinary man is in revolt. His revolt is not political or social. There is little danger of revolution and indeed there is not even a great danger of war. The revolt is not directed against injustice and oppression, but against the stupidity of life. The ordinary man has asked to be shown the meaning of his existence and he has been given a television set. He knows better than his leaders that no real problems are being solved and he is not too proud to ask for help without insisting upon scientific or religious 'orthodoxy' in the source from which it may come.

The help must be simple and effective and these are two of the greatest merits of Subud. We may, therefore, expect that as Subud becomes accessible to the ordinary people of all countries it will appeal to them first.

Here I can report a conversation of Pak Subuh with a small group of influential people in Germany who argued that he should, in the initial stages, restrict the transmission of Subud to those who could 'influence the masses'. They said that such recognized leaders would not wish to share in the latihan with common people lacking in education, but that these latter would quickly follow a lead. They assured Pak Subuh that there was a widespread feeling in Germany that some new spiritual revival must come; and, providing Subud carried the seal of approval of well-known names, it might spread all over Germany like wild-fire.

Pak Subuh replied that he was in any case debarred from rejecting anyone who might come, but that even if this were not so, Subud must rise upon the foundation of the ordinary people. He said that when he was thirty-six years old he had been invited by one of the Rajas of Java to become his adviser in the reorganization of his state. Pak Subuh had refused on the ground that this might separate him from the ordinary people.

The world today needs above all that the ordinary people of every race and nation should regain faith in the Wisdom and Power of God and that trust in Providence should be restored. In this way alone can the 'inner-world forces' be brought into equilibrium with the 'outer-world forces'. We should, therefore, welcome above all else a way and a method that is open to all who ask for it and which can be followed in all conditions of life. Subud requires only helpers who are prepared to carry the burden of transmitting the contact and places in which the latihan can be practised. Its chain reaction will enable it to keep pace with any demand.

8. Concluding Remarks

I must end, as I began, with apologies. I have been too close to the events I have described to be able to present them with the required objectivity. Reading through what I have written, I recognize an enthusiasm that outruns the ascertainable facts. I have tried, in this second edition, to bring out more explicitly the difficulties and the hazards of Subud. These have not engendered doubts in my mind concerning the validity of the main thesis. Among those who by now have gained considerable experience of the latihan are many confirmed sceptics who have been compelled to admit that we are in the presence of a real and continuing action. If we are now more aware of the difficulties than when I first wrote, we also have a far greater weight of evidence that this is no mere flash in the pan.

I will therefore summarize my own impressions and convictions. Firstly, Subud does work. I have not been writing about some ingenious theory as to how mankind could be saved, but about a process that I see working from day to day. Secondly, Subud is supremely easy to enter. It is only required that one should receive the necessary explanations, wait three months and then ask. Everyone that sincerely asks can receive the contact. Thirdly, Subud gives positive results in every sphere of human life: in physical health, in family and social relationships and, most significantly, in the spiritual and religious experience of man. Fourthly, Subud is open to all without restrictions of race, creed or condition. It requires no preparation and no special qualifications. Fifthly, Subud has an unlimited capacity for expansion, and its rate of progress will be limited only by the number of people who ask for the contact.

These are practical points that matter for any earthly undertaking. Subud is more than an earthly undertaking - it is the way to Abodes that are far higher than the earth, and Abodes, moreover, to which we human beings rightly belong.

Subud will expand just as fast as it is God's Will that it should do so. If it is to move very rapidly, indications will be sent that will attract the interests and hopes of many people. If the process is to go slowly, it will pass from friend to friend, from parents to children, until its value is demonstrated by results that cannot be denied. A philosophy is tested by its consistency and adequacy; a moral teaching, by its conformity with our intuitions of right and wrong; a religious dogma by its power to establish and hold the faith of millions. But a *process* can be tested only by results. Subud is a process, and it must submit to the ultimate test: "By their fruits ye shall know them - do men gather grapes of thorns or figs of thistles?"

Chronological list of published books

The list of the Collected Works of J.G. Bennett is of necessity an approximation, for the following reason. The books fall into three categories: first, in **BOLD CAPITALS** – the books written originally for print publication, edited and prepared by the author himself; second, in *Italics* – the books which are formed from transcriptions of orally delivered lectures, either in public or to an invited audience, and edited by the author himself for publication in print after the event; and third, in ordinary script: those titles which were taken from either manuscript or from transcribed lectures, edited and prepared for publication by other people after the death of the author. Since there are still lengthy texts and transcriptions still awaiting evaluation and preparation for possible future publication the list must be regarded as provisional.

1. *The Crisis in Human Affairs*
2. **WHAT ARE WE LIVING FOR?**
3. *Who is Man?*
4. **THE DRAMATIC UNIVERSE VOL. 1: THE FOUNDATIONS OF NATURAL PHILOSOPHY**
5. **CONCERNING SUBUD**
6. **THE DRAMATIC UNIVERSE VOL. 2: THE FOUNDATIONS OF MORAL PHILOSOPHY**
7. **WITNESS**
8. *Towards the True Self in the Approach to Subud*
9. *Christian Mysticism and Subud*
10. *Gurdjieff – A Very Great Enigma*
11. *The Shivapuri Baba and His Message*
12. *Energies*
13. Sunday Talks at Coombe Springs
14. *A Spiritual Psychology*
15. **LONG PILGRIMAGE**
16. *Creative Thinking*

Made in the USA
Middletown, DE
26 May 2019